LOSING FAITH

LOSING FAITH

Those who have walked away . . .

Andy Frost

Authentic

First published 2010 by Authentic Media Limited
Milton Keynes
www.authenticmedia.co.uk

British Library Cataloguing in Publication Data

A catalogue record for this book is available from the
British Library

ISBN-13: 978-1-85078-879-9

Cover design by Phil Miles
Printed and bound in Great Britain by Cox and Wyman, Reading

Dedicated to all who have lost faith . . .

Contents

Acknowledgements

With immense thanks to: David Somers for all of your transcribing and support; Charlotte Hubback, Lindsey Macfarlane and Theresa Malinowska for your insight; and, of course, my beautiful wife Jo.

Introduction

How Peter can deny knowing Jesus baffles me.

The first time, he gives a blunt rebuff, 'I don't know him.'[1]

Then, the disciple replies with an oath, 'I don't know the man.'[2]

And the third time, he calls down curses and swears.[3]

How can he?

After three years of walking, talking, and eating with Jesus? After seeing all the miracles, teachings and healings?

Just before the cockerel crowed, Peter loses faith.

Writing this book has been painful for me, particularly because the issue of losing faith is so raw, and the confusion is so real.

I grew up in south-west London attending a traditional Methodist church. We had a great youth group where about ten of us made commitments to follow Jesus. Fifteen years on, I am the only one who still actively lives out my faith.

I also had friends at university who were heavily involved in the Christian Union. They were passionate about Jesus and they read their Bibles. And yet a few years later, some of them appear to have lost faith.

As I travel the country, I frequently meet mothers who are praying for their children to rediscover their beliefs, men who weep for their friends who have lost theirs, and teenagers who are trying to comprehend why their parents have walked away from Jesus.

Confronted with so many heart-breaking stories, I was forced away from the safety of platitudes and the comfort of clichés. Nothing about the loss of faith is simple.

I came into this writing project with the working title 'backsliders' (we were all certain this could not be the final title), but quickly discovered this term would not adequately describe those whose stories fill these pages. The term refers to people who revert back to old ways; to wrongdoing and sin. It assumes people leave the Christian faith because they are lured back to their previous behaviour. For some, this is true: the bright neon lights of hedonism or materialism pull them away from faith. But falling away from Christianity is not necessarily about the desire to revert to old ways.

Many people ask me if this is another book about individuals who still love Jesus but are bored with church meetings. They ask if the book is about people who haven't lost faith in God but have lost faith in institutions. While this is a valid query, loss of faith is not simply about the way we do church.

The underlying question that keeps arising is '*How* can people walk away from their faith?' Some people tell me those who walk away never really had an authentic relationship with God in the first place. Perhaps that is true for some, but for others, they taste the reality of God, but still leave. For some, it is not even about doubting God's existence, but doubting something of God's character.

People have always walked away from God. They even walked away from Jesus as he walked the earth, when his teaching became too hard. Jesus explained this in a parable about a man who went to sow seeds, some of which sprouted quickly but were strangled by weeds or scorched by the sun. Other seeds fell on good soil and produced a fruitful harvest.

On the one hand, there will always be people who lose faith. However, God calls us and equips us to build faith in one another, to encourage each other to grow in Christ and build the kingdom.

At times we are guilty of doing the exact opposite. We get in the way of another's discipleship rather than helping him or her to live a Jesus-centred life. We have the potential to help people blossom in their relationship with God but we also have the potential to knock people off course. What I have written is not just an exploration of our journeys, but is also, I hope, a prophetic call to action. It is a narrative to reconnect with those that have lost faith, and a call to help build the sort of Christian community that helps faith flourish.

A packet of cookies and everything shifts . . .

The author Douglas Adams tells this story. He arrives early for a train and so pops into a shop to grab a newspaper, a coffee and a packet of cookies. He waits for his train at a table, on which he places his cookies. He sips his coffee and skims the paper.

Sat opposite him is a nondescript man in a suit. Suddenly and unexpectedly, the man leans over grabs the cookies, opens the packet, takes one out and eats it. Adams is shocked. 'They are my cookies,' he thinks, but has no idea how to respond and so just ignores it. He continues skimming the paper and takes a cookie for himself.

He is dumbstruck again as the stranger opposite leans over and helps himself to another cookie. Adams is embarrassed he had not mentioned anything when the man opened the packet initially, so he feels he cannot confront him now. And so Adams just takes another cookie.

The process continues. The stranger takes a cookie . . . then he takes a cookie . . . the stranger takes a cookie . . . he takes a cookie . . . until the packet is empty. At this point, they look at each other and the stranger walks off.

Moments later, Adams gets to his feet to catch his train and discovers his packet of cookies beneath his paper. His entire viewpoint changes in a second: the stranger had not rudely been helping himself to Adams' cookies, Adams had been rudely helping himself to the stranger's cookies.[4]

There are moments in life when our viewpoint suddenly shifts.

You are about to read the stories of people aged between sixteen and thirty-five. While I conducted these interviews and heard first-hand of people's faith journeys I was reminded of the shifts in viewpoints that have occurred over the last couple of decades. Culture has moved on so quickly.

There has been a cultural shift – not only in how society works – but in how people want to live; a cultural shift the church has often unfortunately failed to comprehend. As I immersed myself in these stories of losing faith, I heard a very different viewpoint to the one the church traditionally understands.

In order to comprehend these new perspectives, I had to learn how to listen.

It's not just me that needs to do this. I think many of us are bad at it. We are always waiting for our turn to interject. We hear the sounds the other person is making but we often fail to hear what is actually being said. We want to share our side of the story or our interpretation, especially when it comes to conversations about God.

Some here lost their faith in a moment and there are others who drifted. They have made a hundred small decisions and the rip current of life has led them away from Jesus. Some of them have now returned to faith; others remain distant.

Although good books have been written about the current trends for losing belief, I want to tell you about people's reality: stories not as statistics, but as individuals' lives. I discovered each faith journey is so different. Their stories are like paintings full of texture, created as the painter adds layer upon layer of brushstrokes to the canvas. They are a complex collage of childhood memories and adulthood realities, frustrations and joys, hopes and fears, times of revelation and times of dryness, all overlaid upon one another.

To truly engage with these stories we must be willing to listen humbly. In my interviews I offered no response: I simply listened.

Now, each story surely has another perspective. After a marital breakdown, there are two sides. This is not a police investigation to apportion blame though: this is an opportunity to listen to the unheard voices.

I invite you to earwig on these conversations. Yet I warn you these stories may leave you with more questions than answers; this is not a series of neat responses but reflections over big questions. I encourage you to wrestle with these questions as I do. There is no quick-fix solution to be applied to each individual's experience. There is no simple spiritual to-do list to rekindle faith. What comes through is a challenge to respond to the realities of those leaving their faith; and to effectively encourage those in our current community.

As we explore these big questions, I am encouraged by the fact faith and the potential to connect with God still resonates with the people I meet every day. A New Yorker once challenged Father Henri Nouwen:

> Speak to us about the deepest yearnings of our hearts, about our many wishes, about hope; not about the many strategies for survival, but about trust; not about new methods of satisfying our emotional needs, but about love. Speak to us about a vision larger than our changing perspectives and about a voice deeper than the clamourings of our mass media. Yes, speak to us about something or someone greater than ourselves. Speak to us about . . . God.[5]

I hope *Losing Faith* will give you an insight into a generation who are losing faith but who are longing, knowingly or unknowingly, for an experience of God.

When people lose their faith, the process of rediscovery starts with us. We must listen and begin to understand people's stories. Only then can we journey with them back towards Jesus.

* Please note that some of the names and locations in this book have been changed.

1

The Japanese Hangover

I was running late from an earlier meeting and I hadn't had time to get my head around the forthcoming interview. I quickly used a cash machine and hurried down the street to the coffee shop we had agreed on.

I felt nervous as I automatically weaved my way through the crowds. Meeting a complete stranger, to talk about the intricacies of their faith journey was a daunting task. My mind was crowded with questions. How do I interview whilst remaining pastoral? How would the conversation flow? In fact, would Bethan even open up to me?

A good friend had passed on her details to me a few weeks earlier, having primed her first. And as I approached the coffee shop, I thought of our phone call a few days before. She had seemed keen to help out but uncertain as to whether her story would be of use.

Arriving outside the coffee shop, I examined different faces as I tried to spot Bethan. It dawned on me I had no idea what she looked like, except that she was young. My eyes continued scanning until they suddenly connected with another pair of scanning eyes. Our eyes locked and I asked awkwardly, 'Bethan?'

Almost in unison she asked, 'Andy?' A smile crept across her face and my nerves relaxed.

I could barely see the woman behind the counter through the jars of cookies and muffins. 'Can I get a coke and a . . . What would you like?'

'A green tea,' Bethan responded.

'And one green tea, please.'

The tea shop had large teapots on the wall and bold blue and white striped wallpaper. Bethan found us seats around an old school desk complete with inkwell. She sat opposite me, a pretty girl in her mid twenties with hazel eyes and short brown spiky hair.

She filled me in on her details. She was working in a sales office three days a week but her real passion was her work with women involved in prostitution. Her eyes lit up as she talked about the charity she was employed by. Almost reluctantly, she then began to tell me about her faith.

'I'm from an atheist background,' Bethan began, leaning towards me as she spoke. 'My parents were lawyers and I was brought up very anti-faith. At primary school, everyone else would be playing mummies and daddies and I'd be arguing with my friends about evolution. I was pretty precocious.'

'Then, when I went to a secondary school for girls, I got bullied most of the time. I believed everything the bullies said – at the age of fourteen I really hated myself.'

She spoke softly with a refined accent. The café was buzzing with families with young children and ambient music was cascading down from the stereo speakers. I moved closer so as not to miss what she was saying.

After getting almost straight As at GCSE, Bethan moved to a boys' school, where there were only 20 girls. Overnight she went from being the least popular to the most popular.

'It became about the way I looked,' she explained. Whilst at the girls' school she felt popularity was about personality. And because of that she thought everyone hated her. But then at the boys' school, it all changed. Looks meant popularity and Bethan's beauty caused her now to be loved.

On the outside she was incredibly admired, going to dozens of parties and still gaining top marks. However, beneath this successful surface, she was spiralling out of control: taking slimming tablets and getting so drunk she would pass out. Her boyfriend cheated on her and she developed an eating disorder.

'My parents didn't know at the time, but I told them after I got diagnosed with bulimia, and they thought I was just being melodramatic. I guess they didn't want to believe what was going on. I was still getting As, especially in languages, but I'd grown up speaking them, so I'd just turn up and chat. The only people who knew were my boyfriend and his best friend.'

Things got even worse. Her boyfriend's best friend would inform Bethan when her boyfriend was being unfaithful. One time, as he told her, she became distraught. The friend hugged her. Then he raped her.

'I just froze, I couldn't do anything.'

Bethan could tell I was shocked by her revelation. She was so matter-of-fact. I had not expected her story to take this kind of a twist.

'Are you OK with hearing this?' she questioned over the din of coffee grinders and noisy families.

'Yes, of course,' I said carefully. 'As long as you are happy to talk about it.'

'I always thought if I was in that situation, I would fight like anything, but I just couldn't. I froze. It then happened regularly for about a year. I didn't have any feeling, I just went completely numb. I didn't care what happened to me.'

After a sip of her green tea, Bethan continued. At university, she had stopped looking after herself. She took ecstasy pills and went running in the middle of the night. People used to warn her it was dangerous and she might get raped.

'I didn't care though. I really didn't care at all.'

One morning she woke up and, on the spur of the moment, decided to switch her degree from French and Spanish to Japanese and Spanish. (When she later became a Christian, she came to believe the Holy Spirit had prompted her to do this.) A year or so after this, she went to live in Japan for twelve months.

In Japan, Bethan met a missionary (he was also on her course) who said he felt God had told him to talk to her. She saw something different in him and began opening up. During their conversations, he would try to talk to her about Jesus and how he loves us. Bethan responded that if he actually knew what she had been through he wouldn't see God as loving.

She was, however, intrigued and when he invited her to come to church, she agreed.

'I found church terrifying. I got myself locked in the toilet but I didn't want to ask for help because I was scared of everyone.'

Despite this, Bethan began to pray. She discovered she could pray for her friends but not for herself. And then as she travelled around Japan, she came to a stunningly beautiful place where the mountains dip into the water. In that moment, the penny dropped. This beauty could not be mere chance. 'I knew that day there was a God.'

Soon after Bethan got sick. As she journeyed from one side of Japan to the other, she was given a number of diagnoses, one of which was cancer. She ended up in hospital for an operation and began thinking if there was a God then he was a mean God. Yet concurrently, she found herself praying before the operation and experienced a deep sense of peace for the first time.

Back in the UK, she started dating the missionary guy she had met in Japan. She felt strongly she didn't want to become a Christian just for him but because she believed it herself. So it was while her boyfriend was overseas that she decided to make that personal choice to become a Christian.

Bethan had been attending a large church anonymously. At a gospel appeal there she raised her hand. Though feeling insecure about responding so publicly, she remembers 'the people around me all seemed to disappear and this amazing love overwhelmed me . . . the most amazing feeling . . . I guess it's the first time I'd experienced such a thing and that's when I became a Christian.'

After making the decision she told her mother, which was a big step, as her mother was so anti-Christian. She began to make lifestyle changes and attend church when at university.

Finishing her green tea (a hangover from her time in Japan, she said) she continued, 'While church had been great as I'd heard about grace, coming from my past I had a lot of junk.'

'Then I got sick again and went to hospital with another cyst. After a scan they said they would have to do some serious surgery which would mean I would become infertile. This was devastating.'

Lying in a hospital ward preparing for an emergency operation, Bethan called a Christian friend to pray. Her friend happened to be in a prayer meeting and everyone there joined together in prayer. When she came round from the operation, she was expecting to be told she was infertile. However, the doctors hadn't needed to do the depth of surgery expected. Prayer had worked.

Despite the miraculous, her regular church attendance and her public commitment, Bethan's faith was wavering.

The surgery had gone well, but she was still in pain. She couldn't understand how God would let her suffer in this way. It seemed to contradict the God of love. At the same time, her relationship was in trouble. Her missionary boyfriend said God had told him they could not be together. Bethan was desolate.

She rubbed her temples, as if she had a headache. 'So I'd become a Christian through this guy, but he kept telling me God was saying no to our relationship. It was messy. We were in the same Japanese class at uni, which was a tiny department, so I saw him most days and then he'd come round, say "God says no to us being together" but then kiss me. Over time I got more and more upset by this.'

In many ways it appears Bethan's discovery of God's love was intertwined with her relationship. She remembers eventually turning round to him and snapping, 'Look, don't talk to me, about you, about church, I don't want to hear it.'

Whilst she was struggling with her romantic relationship, she was also struggling in her relationship with the church. 'The church seemed very ill-equipped to cope with me, and I didn't get the support I could've done.' During her finals, she was swamped with work and began skipping church. Some Christian friends lectured her about not going. 'But whenever I went to church, I ended up being the mad woman in the corner crying. I was an emotional wreck and as people started to pray for me, I didn't really know what was going on . . . I was just suddenly really emotional. And I didn't want to be the mad woman.'

Bethan had told people at the church some of her history and she had been through a discipleship course but she had felt it was a process of 'Bring them in, get them through, they'll be OK.' But she was not OK.

She began to feel if she stopped going to church, she could avoid being emotional and having to deal with her past.

'When I graduated, I went out and got off my face and ended up with a non-Christian. The relationship wasn't a positive one. I call it my train-crash relationship. In seeing this guy I was deciding to completely cut God off in my mind.'

Bethan had ceased going to church and given up on her faith.

'There was a girl I met up with called Hannah. She was kind of a mentor figure for a while and I remember saying to her one day, "Look I don't want anything more to do with church." And she said, "Yeah, I understand." People nagging me about church didn't help me at all. But she was honest with me and I valued that, and even through all of this, she wanted to hang out anyway. It was like this unconditional love that was really heart-warming. She was such a good example to watch. Other people would stop calling me, but she didn't. I felt when I'd stopped going to church other people stopped caring and I didn't hear much from anyone else.'

Having graduated, Bethan went to work in Japan on an HIV AIDS project. She deliberately took no Bible: her faith was finished with. Yet, as she was waiting at the airport, Hannah sent her a text: 'Don't stop looking for God; he'll never stop looking for you.'

The discipleship factory

Jesus said these words, 'Therefore go and make disciples . . .' (Mt. 28:19).

As the church we can be quite good at helping people make a decision to follow Jesus. However, the issue is we are not called to 'Go make people who say a one-off prayer.' We are called to make disciples – and a key factor for those losing their faith is failed discipleship.

I remember running a mission alongside a number of local churches. The mission was focused on young people and by the end of the week there were fifty or so teenagers who had committed their lives to Jesus. It was such an exciting week.

One year later, I returned to find not one of the fifty was still following Jesus. The discipleship process had not worked. I was gutted.

So what is discipleship?

The term discipleship is the 'process that takes place within accountable relationships over a period of time for the purpose of bringing believers to spiritual maturity in Christ. Biblical examples suggest discipleship is both relational and intentional, both a position and a process.'[6]

What is important in this definition is that as soon as someone makes a commitment of faith, they become a disciple and begin a journey of transformation as they grow to know God better.

The aim is to help people mature in their relationship with Christ beyond a basic prayer, empowering them to disciple others and effectively engage with the world. But I have a confession to make . . .

Discipleship is hard, discipleship is costly and discipleship is time-consuming. Perhaps that is why we often fail at it.

Discipleship smacks hard against a contemporary culture that puts self first. As C.S. Lewis writes, 'Christ says, "Give me All. I don't want so much of your time and so much of your money and so much of your work: I want

You. I have not come to torment your natural self, but to kill it. No half-measures are any good."[7]

We can learn from Bethan's story. She had been through a discipleship course, she was attending church regularly and yet she was not being successfully discipled. She was struggling with the concept of suffering, she was dealing with a romantic relationship God appeared to be breaking up and she was carrying so much baggage that at church all she could do was cry.

Discipleship is such a complex process and in order to make it more manageable, we often just put people through a discipleship programme and expect the finished article to come out at the end. Discipleship is now a process – almost as if disciples were like beef-burgers made on a conveyor belt in McDonald's.

One of the gravest dangers with this conveyor belt approach is we begin to see people as numbers rather than individuals loved by God. It is painful to hear how many of Bethan's church friends stopped calling when she abandoned her faith.

Burgers can be made through a simple formulaic process but disciples can not.[8] Each of us is so different. We have different backgrounds, different experiences, different abilities, different questions, different needs and a one-size-fits-all discipleship scheme is not going to work.

Over the years I have witnessed many different styles of discipleship programme. I remember as a child going to Saturday morning Bible classes at the local Methodist church, complete with exams. (That really made me love church!) The concept was that with enough good Bible knowledge, information would drift from my head to my heart and my lifestyle would change.

You may rarely hear of Bible clubs like this today but we still hold onto this top-down approach, of trying to input truth and doctrine into a new Christian without understanding where they are at. We do this in our follow-up courses after missions and sometimes even our mentorship schemes are based solely on passing down theological insights and keeping people in check rather than hearing the individual's story.

These models can have a certain amount of success but they are all 'top-down' in their method. They rub up against a younger generation: this generation has experienced a school system that celebrates everyone's right to question and to share opinions. They, therefore, need that same flexibility in their discipleship.

Bethan had some powerful issues to be resolved if she was going to be able to move forward in her journey with God. In particular, sexual abuse is a huge obstacle to deal with when you are trying to understand 'God is love'. Bethan is not an exception. We live in a society where there is so much abuse and unhealthy experimentation. Disparate issues such as pornography, casual sex and bullying are common in this generation. There are many habits and memories needing to be dealt with.

Relational and intentional

The definition of discipleship earlier uses the terms relational and intentional. These are crucial. Many of our discipleship programmes are intentional but they lack relationship. We have taken the words of the Great Commission 'teaching them to obey everything I have commanded you' and presumed teaching means sitting people down in rows and giving talks.

Jesus taught as he welcomed children, as he prayed for the sick, as he ate meals, as he wept, as he turned over tables – and as he preached. Jesus was relational. For me, being relational is more than being sat in the same room, being relational is about understanding one another. Being relational is about hearing those questions and needs rather than guessing or pre-supposing which pieces of theology need to be taught.

Traditional forms of discipleship are too prescriptive and formalized, based almost entirely on head knowledge. They lack practical application. We don't challenge cultural values. We don't talk about lifestyle choices. We don't teach people how to listen to God. We just cram people's heads with theological concepts.

Our biblical insights should be embodied and communicated through everyday life: we don't shy away from teaching these truths but we share these insights as and when people are ready to hear them. Discipleship should be a *dialogue built upon relationship*.

However, at the same time, it is easy to drink coffee and share life together but to lose the intentionality of discipleship. Relational, yes: but we must also be intentional, making it clear that when we spend time, we are doing so with the aim of knowing God more fully. Jesus said 'For where two or three come together in my name, there am I with them' (Mt. 18:20). Jesus including the words 'in my name' brings intentionality here.

It is hard work discipling. Our programmes and courses are undemanding options as opposed to the time-consuming and difficult task of helping others, especially when they may have painful pasts or come from a different background. It might be arduous but as Christians, we need to all be at work discipling others. I find it fascinating that as Jesus gives the Great Commission, some doubted. Jesus even commissioned the doubters.

I preach in local Methodist chapels and I have met some incredibly faithful people of God. But I have also met many people who have been attending church for a lifetime but who have never been taught to pray out loud, who have never been taught how to read the Bible themselves or who have never learnt God wants to use their lives. It is heartbreaking. Maybe we are partly failing to disciple new believers because many churchgoers have never been discipled themselves.

Bethan was being discipled but part of her struggle was this was being done, at least in part, by her boyfriend. Her faith was being built awash with emotions when he ended their relationship, announcing it was God's will. Discipleship confused with romantic interest can be enormously damaging.

Bethan became embarrassed about going to church. She couldn't stop crying and she felt an emotional wreck. As we disciple, and as people discover more of God, the healing process begins. This journey is not always easy. The healing process involves spiritual heart surgery and it appears God was trying to soothe the wounds from Bethan's history. A church service is perhaps not the best time for this though. Maybe we rush people rather than providing space to pray through issues at another time? Time must be set aside for counselling, prayer and healing.

As Bethan chose to leave her faith behind, she left all Christian community – except for Hannah. When people leave our churches, when they lose their faith, do we maintain a relationship or do we just watch them slip out quietly through the back door? Hannah decided to commit to her relationship with Bethan.

Organic

Factory processes are simple. Personalized discipleship is so much harder.

And the question remains: how do we practically help to disciple others? Discipleship must be relational and intentional – OK. Discipleship shouldn't be squeezed in to an hour-long session once a week – OK. What does discipleship therefore look like?

I understand modern-day life isn't best suited to wandering the country with a group of disciples, meeting with women at wells, having discussions with Pharisaic leaders and depending on others for food and accommodation. I understand this would not really complement the nine-to-five and getting the kids to bed on time.

I am not asking you to roam around in sandals like Jesus but I am asking you to share life like Jesus: sharing meals, sharing dropping the kids at school, sharing how you juggle your finances, sharing your reflections on the news, sharing your stories from work: sharing life. And to do so, maybe we need to live more simply, to carve out time to teach all the things he commanded.

Locally, I have wrestled with the whole issue of discipleship in my Christian community. Together, we opted for a different approach completely. Each of us committed to writing down some goals for the year under the titles of prayer, Bible reading, character, mission and spiritual disciplines. As a community we look to support each other to achieve those goals, helping disciple one another. Each of us, with our very different capacities, personalities, learning styles and stages of faith, are seeking to grow in Christ collectively.

Reading the Bible and grasping theology is vital, a foundational part of discipleship, but it must be made real and practical. Willard, who writes on spiritual formation, believes we need to help new Christians take 'small but effective steps by which he or she will quite certainly be met by God to accomplish the amazing works of spiritual formation in Christ-likeness.'[9]

Discipleship should thus equip disciples to engage with God, allowing them to find a practical and living faith.

As a Christian community we have also wanted to draw on the rich traditions of the church, using the more contemplative ways of engaging with God, such as pilgrimage. Many of these lost practices allow us to reflect on the biblical story not only with our minds, but with our bodies. Discipleship is about engaging fully with Scripture and the story of Jesus.

I wonder if Bethan had been offered some alternative forms of discipleship, she may have held onto her faith. I wonder if her faith would have been more constant if she had been offered more than a course, if she had been offered prayer outside of the Sunday service and if she had had someone other then her boyfriend discipling her.

Discipleship is not a predictable, measurable process. And it is by being relational and intentional that we help to create an environment rather than a process . . . an environment that sees people as individuals rather than numbers.

Friends not projects?

I am sure there are many people like Bethan who knew God but chose to leave him behind. When they lose faith, we must not become nagging siblings, persistently demanding they come to church, neither should we desert them.

Hannah did not desert Bethan when Bethan deserted her faith. Hannah made herself available. She listened to where she was at, even understanding some of what she was going through – and then she sent her that pithy text, 'Don't stop looking for God; he'll never stop looking for you.'

And God didn't.

In Japan, a country with little Christian heritage, where Bethan had no Bible and no Christian community, Bethan rediscovered her faith.

It was about six months' later. 'I got to Japan and God revealed himself to me. I met him in a real way and fell in love with him. He became my dad when I was there. I became so desperate for love and kept asking, "What is love?"'

She went on to explain in vivid detail how she learnt to hear God's still voice. She experienced feeling trapped in bed by demons one night but God taught her to use Scripture in spiritual warfare. 'I remember waking up in the morning and thinking, "Wow, so it's real then!" I'd go running in the mountains in the morning and worship God, I was completed bowled over in love with him, spending all my spare time worshipping and learning: it was pretty amazing.'

She paused, memory clouding her features.

Her story was not a smooth transition. She came back from Japan early as her aunt was sick. Back home in Cardiff, she had no Christian contacts. Hannah was in Birmingham. She began dating the same non-Christian and felt God had become distant. It was much easier compromising her faith around her non-Christian friends. A few months after this, she felt God's tug and decided to end her relationship with her boyfriend. Once again, she knew God's presence.

It was at this time Bethan got angry. The buried pain resurfaced and she would have to grasp railings on the tube tightly to prevent herself from hitting men looking at explicit images of women. She found a new church where two women regularly met with her to pray and speak prophetically into her life. With frightening flash-backs, the healing process began.

It excites me how God is using Bethan today. Although she went through horrific experiences, God is redeeming her story as she helps sex workers discover worth and meaning.

Reflecting on her account, one thing is certain: discipleship is not easy. Although God could disciple us independently, he has for some purpose built us into a church where we can help one another along the journey, as co-pilgrims.

'Looking back,' Bethan said, 'the fact Hannah didn't ram Christianity down my throat, that she still wanted to know me, even when I running in the opposite direction, meant I was a friend not a project.'

When people leave their faith, we can easily become disillusioned but what had been sown in Bethan's life was not wasted. It is now bearing fruit. Sometimes although we can give up, God has not given up. And even when we make mistakes with our pieces of the jigsaw, God is still in control of the whole box. Let's have less projects and more relationships.

Practical tips

- Stay committed to people who have left their faith even though they may never return.
- Make yourself available to talk about faith without being forceful.
- Remember God is at work and has not given up, so neither should you! Allow this to guide your prayers.

2

Smell the Coffee

It was an ancient pub and as I waited for Jane, I wondered whether this was the best venue for our conversation. The décor was from a bygone era and the smell of stale beer emanated from the cushioned seats in the summer heat.

Despite the muted drone of traffic from the road outside, the pub was at least quiet. Jane walked in, quickly spotting me. It wasn't hard as the only other customers were two elderly gentlemen sporting top hats.

Her blue top matched her blue eyeliner and her skirt was imprinted with images of Elvis Presley; it swung around her slender frame as she sat down. She wore a chunky white necklace, setting off her tan. In her mid twenties, Jane had grown up in the suburbs of London. Her mum was an evangelical Christian, her dad wasn't. She grew up attending church weekly with her mum and her brother.

Jane's expression grew earnest as she divulged the depths of her faith experience to me over a drink. She remembered herself as a six year old who believed deeply in God and prayed every day. One day her mother asked if she wanted to invite Jesus into her heart, but Jane couldn't understand why she had to do this officially when she already clearly believed. 'Doesn't he know?' she thought to herself.

Jane animatedly elaborated on her background. Her mother had done an array of jobs. Her father was a mechanical engineer. They had met before Jane's mother had become a Christian.

Church was a substantial part of Jane's childhood memories despite her father's lack of faith. Thinking about this she began to play with her necklace. 'I think when you're a kid you just accept things. You don't really question.'

She knew her father had had negative experiences growing up and attending a Catholic school. His upbringing had been strict and he'd been caned for not going to school. Jane accepted him as a scientific person who thought in a linear way.

As is often the case with young adults, Jane stopped going to church when she was twelve as there wasn't anyone else there her age. She wanted Sunday mornings to herself.

She explained how church had become boring and full of people to whom she couldn't relate. Her mother would come home from church feeling angry, and take it out on the family. There was no youth work provision and Jane felt like a token young person, expected to wear a pretty dress.

'Although I'd stopped going to church, I decided when I was about fifteen, that I would go on this weekend with the crazy church Mum was still a part of.' There she had a real experience of the Holy Spirit. The new youth worker prayed for her and kept saying how much Jesus loved her. She became extremely emotional – not one of her usual characteristics.

Jane felt like something was taking place, but it was confusing as no-one talked about it with her. Looking back now, she says she can explain her spiritual experiences with psychology, but is still confused about what happened.

After some time away, Jane eventually decided she wanted to get back involved with church, as there was a sense of rootedness in it. She soon found a new church with people her own age and felt she had become her own person, no longer seen as her mother's daughter. She had found the church through a school friend and started spending two nights a week there: Friday nights were social evenings and Sunday nights were spent discussing Christianity. The youth group community enabled her faith to develop.

'So when you chose to go back to church, how was your mum?' I asked.

Jane looked thoughtful. 'I don't remember her reaction. I think she was quite pleased. She was supportive and she said she saw changes in my life. It made me more confident.' Jane continued to experience the Holy Spirit at events and festivals and that continually gave her a desire to explore more of God. Despite this she had a separate lifestyle of getting drunk and partying discordant with the rest.

At eighteen, she took a gap year doing volunteer youth work and the binge drinking stopped as she became more serious about her relationship with God. Pushing back her brown hair from her face, she described how the youth worker job in Leicestershire was tough, but it taught her who she was. Leading a youth group in an Anglican church was just one of the many responsibilities she had: 'Whatever was going on in the church, I was organizing it.'

Despite the role being a huge responsibility, having no money and being lonely, her confidence grew.

After a gap year, Jane moved on to study Psychology and Art at university. She had a firm resolve to live out her faith and was really active in the Christian Union, running Alpha courses and going to small groups. She reminisced about being upset that she was not chosen to go on the CU Executive Committee. The CU became her expression of church, when she had failed to settle in a local church in the town.

Trying to dig deeper and discover more of Jane's relationship with God at the time, I asked, 'So were you reading the Bible and praying?'

'Yeah, I was quite full on,' she began, 'but then I began to get stressed out at uni.' She started suffering from panic attacks and depression – yet she carried on praying even though it was a tough time. God seemed silent, but it didn't stop her being active.

Jane described the panic attacks. During this time, she felt her Christian friends let her down. Her friends who had no faith supported her in practical ways and she began to feel distant from her Christian community.

At the same time, her course in psychology was making her look at things in a new light: in particular, her identity, her history and her family. Although these reflections did not stop her believing, she began to see things differently, especially some of her experiences of God.

On finishing university Jane returned to London. She recovered from the panic attacks but began to find Christian thought processes damaging. She'd learnt if you go to church and believe, then God will bless you and help you through. However, in reality, trying to live a life pleasing to God was adding stress.

Jane sought help from Christians but found they often over-spiritualized issues. She explained, 'One woman thought I was demon-possessed and that really messed things up again. I had no idea what to believe and stopped going to church. Church had become quite stressful. I decided to put Christianity on a shelf in order to get better.'

I asked if it was then she lost her faith, trying to say it in a gentle way.

Jane's story was not as clear-cut as that. She went back to a different church once the panic attacks had subsided. In her new church she discovered one of the church leaders was hitting on a friend.

Jane confronted the leader. He became incredibly defensive, arguing it was his business. What cut her to the quick was his remark, 'I don't need your respect or trust.'

The following day, she spent the morning crying. Her mother asked her about it, and when she told her, her mother said, 'It happened at our church too.'

The hurt evident on Jane's face, she related how her mother said the minister had made passes at her, and many other women at the church. The first time, he was forgiven, but then it happened again and again.

Her mother's confession revealed the truth behind the anger after church when Jane was younger. For Jane it was the final nail in the coffin. 'When I found out about the minister, I was like, bam, I'm walking away, that's it. I had seen the church as a dangerous place . . .'

Warts and all?

And they all lived happily ever after . . .

As a child, I used to love fairy tales. No matter how bad the story got, there was always a happy ending. And everybody loves a happy ending.

When I was nineteen, I worked in the Lake District in a hotel for the summer. During my time there, one of the front-of-house staff, a churchgoer for many years, became a Christian. He was bubbling with joy. It was amazing to see.

However, a few weeks after he had made that commitment, he turned round and said to me, 'You didn't warn me that life would still be difficult.'

I was taken aback. In the process of leading him to Christ I had inadvertently given him the impression he would live happily ever after. I had not set out to hide the hardships of following Christ or the fact that believers still have to go through the reality of life, but somehow he had presumed a fairy-tale ending.

See, there is a fairy-tale ending that lasts for eternity but right here on earth (although we begin to live in that eternity now) life is hard. In fact, Jesus promises us persecution and hardship. He asks us to pick up our cross and follow him.

Jane seems to have been sold the 'happy ever after' fairy tale. She knew life was not perfect but painful church hypocrisy had been hidden from her. She had not been given the tools to deal with the tough situations when the miraculous one-prayer-fixes-all formula fails.

To borrow one of Jesus' phrases, Jane discovered dead men's bones and everything unclean behind the façade of beautiful whitewashed tombs (Mt. 23:27). Her story is an introduction to the 'warts and all' side of church: the side of church we don't like to talk about.

We don't like to admit everything is not perfect. On a Sunday morning we want to be one big happy family with perfect game-show-host smiles. We want our churches to be places where the drug addict beats addiction and never lapses again; where the former adulterer remains pure forever; and where the ex-prisoner overcomes his anger and is meek and mild from then on.

Yet sometimes our churches are not quite so perfect . . . people fall from grace. And often we try to cover it up. We bury real issues for fear that if the world discovers the church is not faultless, it might undermine the gospel. However, when the issues finally work their way to the surface, we discover we have weakened the gospel by trying to cloak our painful shortcomings in secrecy.

It's easy when you hear stories like Jane's, to think it is just somewhere else. We believe it could never happen at our church. But the truth is churches are full of 'recovering sinners'. Things go wrong, sometimes spectacularly.

We discovered an issue of abuse in a church I was helping to lead. It blew my mind. I never thought these kinds of concerns could invade our happy little community. I naively thought as long as people were worshipping Jesus on a Sunday morning then everything was fine.

As the church, we need to face the reality we are living in a broken world. It's tough when a church member fails but it is even more painful when a church leader does so.

Jane respected her two leaders. She trusted them. Yet her struggling faith could not withstand the blow of discovering their failings. In a moment of revelation, her beliefs finally unravelled.

These men had preached excellent sermons. They had told stories of God working wonders. They had prayed with much authority. And yet they had also made serious mistakes – mistakes that had been covered up or ignored. Jane's expectations were dashed and she was left disillusioned.

One of the most dangerous things we do is to put our leaders on pedestals. We presume because they have been to Bible college or because they wear a dog collar they are somehow insusceptible to the intoxicating grasp of sin. We fail to recognize they, too, are human.

I have several friends who are pastors and it saddens me when they say they cannot truly be themselves around their congregation. They feel pressurized to be professional, perfect men of God and are unable to talk honestly about their struggles and their failings. I can understand you would not want your pastor to have a crisis of faith in the pulpit on Sunday morning but the idea leaders feel they cannot be themselves is dangerous: it encourages insincerity.

Too often, we seek godly role models and we pin our hopes on them. Instead, we should be pinning our hopes squarely on Jesus. There is nothing wrong with having role models but we must realize they are not perfect – they are human like us.

Jane's story throws out a whole host of uncomfortable questions for the church. How do we show grace and forgiveness whilst protecting the congregation? How do we deal with church leaders who mess up in spectacular style? Do we publicly reveal it or do we hide it under the carpet? Do we confess the fairy-tale ending is not yet a reality?

We regularly study biblical leaders who failed in their struggles with lust, pride and integrity: like the worshipper King David, who had a heart after God. Yet we somehow find it surprising when it happens to our leaders today.

Silence

Jane's story is not just about church leadership. Suffering is another significant thread in it. The panic attacks, stress and depression she experienced are becoming an ever-common occurrence in our pressurized society.

Mental illness of all types is often grossly misunderstood, especially in church. The fact Jane felt she had to stop going to church in order to get better, lays a real challenge to us all. We need to explore how can we support, rather than marginalize, those with mental health issues.

It would be interesting to know how Jane's story would have turned out had she been supported by her Christian friends at her CU and then by her church back home. Community can be an important part of the healing process but instead she felt ostracized, particularly when she was labelled demon-possessed.

If you do believe in demonic activity, it is clear this must be handled incredibly sensitively. If not, we risk alienating the individual. Too often, in certain circles, we over-spiritualize situations and look for a quick fix: a quick prayer that will set everything right again. In Jane's case, there was a lack of provision to help her on the path to recovery.

With stress and depression at epidemic levels the church has an amazing opportunity to offer holistic care. Perhaps if we could overcome some of our hang-ups over mental illness, we could provide qualified support not only to our congregations but to our local communities as well.

On top of the depression, Jane felt God had gone silent.

As I listened to Jane's story I was surprised by how much of her faith had been built upon charismatic spiritual encounters. She talked fondly about Holy Spirit moments. These experiences of God are crucial. The Holy Spirit does not just give us gifts for service, but transforms our character, as the great disciple. Yet God has also given us the Bible.

Do we convey a shallow understanding of God based on experience? Without biblical grounding, do we convey a shallow understanding of God based in experience? Do we sometimes base our relationship with God on mountain-top experiences rather than on a daily devotional life? Do we fail to disciple so that holy encounters are matched with a biblical depth? In certain streams of churchmanship we are marvellous at helping people swim in the rivers of the Holy Spirit but we fail to teach people to dig wells in the wilderness.

It was when Jane began studying psychology that she questioned her interpretations of her experiences. Experiences that had previously been interpreted in a church setting were now being explored with social theories. Yet suffering with depression truly challenged these experiences and her belief in a personal God.

In Pete Greig's book, *God on Mute*, he explores the theology of unanswered prayer; the seasons when God appears to be silent. He perceptively writes,

> Christians are quick to spread glory stories, but disappointments tend to be brushed under the carpet because we don't want to discourage anyone at church or be a bad commercial at work. But God isn't like us. He doesn't get insecure about His performance, and he never asks us to cover up for Him.[10]

The fairy tale suggests everything will be OK but the reality is much harder.

I read Pete's book just before my father was diagnosed with cancer. Within five months my father died. I'll never forget the confused questioning I was wracked with inside and how some people would give me trite answers. While things like 'He's in a better place now' are true, they fail to recognize the need to lament and to grieve. It is tragic that sometimes all the church can offer is an insensitive happy-clappy sing-song when people are yearning for space to engage with God in their reality.

As we gather together as Christians, we must speak into the reality of life's situations rather than maintaining this positive façade. God is at work when we are suffering just as much as when we are laughing: we need to make space for how things actually are.

Jane wanted reality. When she began suffering with depression, she wanted to know the reality of God in her situation. She didn't want to pretend anymore. And when she discovered what had gone on with her church leader in the past, the façade came crashing down. She had been sold a fairy tale – confess Christ and live happily ever after – but one day she smelt the coffee.

The blame game

We live in a blame culture. 'Where there's blame, there's a claim,' as the TV advert says.

Many pin their blame for their loss of faith at the door of the church: hypocrisy . . . being judgemental . . . double standards . . . a lack of reality . . . whatever it may be.

It is easy to be angry with the church. The church is a huge faceless institution. We can all lay blame at faceless institutions. Yet when we make our problem an institution, we become powerless to overcome the hurt and the pain.

If people like Jane are ever going to rediscover their Christian faith, then we will need to help them forgive those who have let them down so they can move on: it is not just about forgiving an institution but about forgiving the very real people who have failed them.

Jane will need to forgive the church minister who acted inappropriately. She will need to forgive the adults in her church who failed to deal properly with the minister and she will need to forgive the church leader who said he did not need her trust. She will need to forgive those who failed to help her in her depression.

So often I hear people tell me they hate The Church – that The Church has hurt them. It is not The Church that has hurt them though, but individuals within a specific church. An institution is not capable of hurting us and causing us to hate it: it is people within it. The institution of the church need not be forgiven – instead we must go through the much more tangible and painful process of forgiving the individuals who have tarnished the name of the church.

If we are to help people come back to God we must preach and live a gospel of hope, based in the reality of a broken world.

According to social scientists, this current generation of twenties and thirties desperately want authenticity. Perhaps one of the quickest ways to help create a more honest church is to encourage and support our leaders to live out an authentic faith based in the harsh reality of life. No fairy tale: just the daily reality of a God who listens – of a God who loves us – of a God who is with us on a mundane weekday morning. I just hope I, too, can live this authentic life with integrity as I pick up my cross and follow Jesus.

On the shelf

I watched the melting ice cubes jump in the glass as Jane put it down. It seemed like such a quick decision. 'So where do you stand now with Christianity? What has happened since that point?' I asked tentatively.

Jane said she has left her faith on the shelf. The only time she talks about it is to share anecdotes.

Her Christian friends reacted with anger and disappointment when she lost her faith and she has now lost contact with many of them.

She is still having therapy and has just started talking through her former faith. 'I think there is a part of me that is still very much Christian but I don't have the energy to live the life. I don't see the point. It seems like you're sacrificing so much for God . . .' Her psychology training made her feel she was conditioned into believing – but at the same time she finds it hard to write it off. Her faith was a key part of her life and she can't seem to lose it fully. 'I can't quite wash my hands of it, and whether it is just the history or whether it's God, I'm not quite sure.'

She went on to tell me how she had felt God had spoken to her at university about marrying a boy from her gap year. During her university years she had refused to date anyone else as she waited for him. Years later, they are now in a relationship.

'So you still have a strange thought God might be on your case?' I asked.

'Perhaps . . .' Jane gazed thoughtfully into the middle distance. 'I may one day change my mind or begin exploring things again, but right now I don't have that desire – there's been too much hurt.'

We said our goodbyes, and I fervently prayed she would start looking for God again one day.

Practical tips

- Don't over spiritualize what is going on in other people's lives.
- Be honest about the reality of following Jesus – both the joys and the difficulties.
- Help friends to pinpoint their specific issues and reasons for losing faith.

3

Cool Christianity

'And I took out the ring leader. I suddenly became cool.'

It is strange how everything can change in an instant. For Kris, this was the moment he began to drift away from God.

Minutes earlier we had peered out of the wide window and watched the stormy ocean that filled the view. The sound of pounding waves could be heard clearly as mountains of white water surged towards the beach. We sat down in the safe confines of the apartment, both dragging our attention away from the surf. I fiddled with the dictaphone and pressed record.

Kris sat opposite me on a bed that doubled as a sofa. He oozed a laid-back attitude, epitomized by his fashionable beard and loose fitting checked shirt, which hid his branded belt and the top of his Quiksilver trousers. Kris's surf-weathered thirty-something face was focused as he prepared to talk.

His story began in childhood. A Christian family. A local Baptist church. Fun Christian summer camps. Important memories of his mother's baptism. A picture of the perfect Christian family unit.

To get below his smooth surface, I asked what his understanding of God was as a child. He became even more focused as he pondered for a moment, stroking his beard. Kris found it hard to recall, but remembered he had believed in and loved God. His faith was very much related to his relationship with his parents.

As he continued to tell his story, I could see him mentally re-playing episodes of his life in his head, dredging up memories abandoned to the depths of time.

Sent to a highly traditional boarding school in Scotland at the age of ten, he had to attend church twice a week (wearing a kilt) and kept his faith for the first few years there. The other children were also from Christian backgrounds, but none would have called themselves Christians. There wasn't a CU or a place for young Christians, just a top-down Scottish High Church but Kris built a good relationship with the chaplain. He also sang in the choir. However, he was getting bullied.

Kris collected his thoughts for a moment. He continued slowly, recalling he wouldn't fight back because he'd always been told to turn the other cheek. The bullying continued for two years. 'One evening when some cool kids in the same year were bullying me and throwing snowballs at me, rage got the better of me . . .' he paused, 'and I took out the ring leader.'

'The next day I became cool and coolness went to my head. Up until that point I had never been cool. All through school I had been bullied and suddenly it changed.'

So the fear of being bullied meant that you jacked in your faith?

'No, it wasn't fear. It was the thrill of being cool and getting girls. I guess I wanted to be accepted by my peers . . . and . . . well . . . going through the changes you go through as a teenager isn't easy. In the midst of it all there was still some faith.'

Kris leant back on the bed, propping himself up on his elbows. I asked what happened to his relationship with the chaplain. He sat up again and told me he had got heavily into drinking, smoking and drugs in the last year at school. Despite this he still had a relationship with the chaplain throughout this rebellious time. He was confirmed because the confirmation classes took place at the Catholic girl's school. Then, as he continued to rebel, eventually he lost his faith.

'At the same time my parents' faith went on the back burner for a few years. They moved to Canada and they never went to church.' Kris paused as he reflected on what he had just said. He had stumbled across a personal revelation, 'I never asked them about this though.' Again he hesitated, frowning. 'Faith for the whole family was put on hold. My sister and I both went off the rails – but I still had to go to church at school, and this was a real bugbear. Church three times a week with dreary messages and dull hymns – everyone begrudged it.'

There was always an element of liking the church deep down, but he wanted to be strong on his own and didn't need God. The chaplain was a skier and Kris had spent some time skiing with him. The chaplain never talked about God outside of church services and didn't come across as a religious man. It was the religious side of church Kris didn't get along with. He reflected how he might have been more affected by the church had it been more relational.

So you feel as though you weren't given the opportunity to develop your own personal faith?

'Yeah, I guess. Looking back, I reckon if I hadn't been sent to boarding school, I would have kept my Christianity. My parents would have inputted spiritually which would have helped.'

After boarding school Kris went to university and got into drug culture, which took him even further away from God. He began to adopt a strange form of spirituality, and following university he moved to the mountains to ski and party.

And God? Did he have any part in your life?

'Nope, just skiing and partying.'

There was a moment of silence as we both listened to the sound of the surf pounding on the beach.

Kris's story reminded me greatly of my own. My Christian family background was excellent but as I went through adolescence, I too struggled. One of the key issues was the top-down church of which Kris spoke. His acknowledgement of the changes you go through as a teenager spoke to me clearly – the need to be accepted – the desire to be cool.

'Coolhunters', Starbucks and the iPod

Kris also kept mentioning the term 'cool'. When he became 'cool' he left the church.

This kind of comment fascinates me. Can church ever be cool? Was Jesus cool? In fact, what is cool?

We can easily think of people who are cool, such as James Dean, Kurt Cobain or Brad Pitt, but it is formidable to define the word.

Malcolm Gladwell writes about his time hanging out with the 'coolhunters', people who are employed by large retail and advertising companies to discover future trends in cool. He draws three observations from his experiences: that cool is continually moving on as soon as it is discovered; that cool cannot be manufactured; and that cool can only be observed by those who are cool.[11] The idea of cool is therefore complex and elusive.

Sometimes, as Christians, we think with the perfect concoction of cool music and cool preachers in an aesthetically cool building, growth is inevitable. But I have an issue with this. We are called to be counter-cultural and our communities should always be formed of an eclectic mix of ages, backgrounds and levels of 'coolness' (as it is perceived by the world).

For me, 'cool' is being real about who we are. It is about knowing who God has called you to be and it is about living it out without a façade.

The issue for Kris was he could not be himself in the church culture surrounding him.

Kris is a risk taker. His passion for adventure is epitomised in his freestyle skiing. And yet in the church context at his boarding school, a Christian faith full of pioneering adventure and 'fullness of life' was not demonstrated (Jn. 10:10). The culture was about safety and structure, not about risk and mission.

Our church culture stops people from finding their identity and their place in God's plans.

Management writer, Charles Handy, believes every organization has a culture.[12] Now the church doesn't categorize itself as an organization (we are a community seeking to follow a way of life together) but the story of Apple, who have become synonymous with the term cool, might help us understand the role of culture. Cameron and Quinn use this example to illustrate how organizations shift from a culture of flexibility and innovation to a culture of stability and control.[13]

Steve Jobs and Steve Wozniak set up Apple, building their first computer in their parents' garages. They made personal computers for young, dynamic Californians. Jobs was a charismatic entrepreneur and, as Apple developed, the pair became known as renegades. The

Apple brand grew and the team began to grow. Apple demonstrated a culture all about pioneering and the freedom to be creative.

They were soon selling thousands of computers and had to increase their distribution channels. Their size meant they needed policies and regulations. As values shifted Jobs was ousted. By the 1990s, the computer industry had moved forward and Apple no longer had innovative computers. The organization now had a culture of stability and control.

Kris was also part of an organization demonstrating a similar culture of stability and control. The church had efficient systems – services that ran on time, a rota for the flower arranging, a choir that had rehearsed, and even a dress code – but in becoming so stable and safe, it had lost any innovative ethos.

The Apple story doesn't finish with their demise. In the late nineties, Jobs was re-employed by Apple. The iPod was birthed. Apple had not only been rescued but was thriving.

This transition through different cultures is not only about individual churches but about denominations too. When the Church of England became too focused on stability and control, an innovator, John Wesley, helped birth Methodism. When Methodism became too focused on stability and control, an innovator, William Booth, helped birth the Salvation Army.

It's not that we must lose all structure and rid ourselves of all stability but we must never stop being creative and innovative. Often, what begins as a movement becomes an organization in order to meet the needs of growth. It then shifts from being an organization to being an institution and before too long, it is a museum. Perhaps with some of our church buildings, we should put a sign up outside saying 'Museum' and charge an entry price to come and view life as it would have been two hundred years ago.

To change our church culture, we simply need to reconnect with the values Jesus exemplified: values like grace; listening to the needs of the world; a passion for justice; and commitment to the kingdom. We need to demonstrate the church is not an old-fashioned institution hidden away in historic buildings but alive and active.

Even mainstream businesses have to work hard to keep their companies focused on their values. The chairman of Starbucks, Howard Schultz, recognizes this. In order to grow their business they had had to make decisions which led to the 'watering down of the Starbucks experience'. In the desire for efficiency they lost something. He concludes, 'Let's get back to the core. Push for innovation and do the things necessary to once again differentiate Starbucks from all others.'[14]

These words ring true for the church today. We need to get back to the core – to the Good News – to enabling people like Kris to find faith and be propelled into the world to live it out.

How have we reduced the most exciting missional movement in history to an archaic institution? Robert Capon argues the biggest threat to the Christian faith is the very fact we have forgotten the Good News: 'Jesus doesn't change people into wide-eyed radicals anymore, He changes them into "nice people."'[15]

We have stopped being a movement stunned by God's grace.

If Kris had been given space to engage, an opportunity to input, a taste of mission and adventure, then perhaps he would never have lost his faith? As Apple invented the iPod, the church needs to create space for innovation, to disciple a new generation that wants a movement and not a museum.

Safety first?

I am not sure I would have turned out as I did if it had not been for the opportunities offered to me. The defining moments in my faith journey have been when people have taken risks on me, allowing me to step into my calling.

At eighteen I worked on a summer camp in the States. Although my faith was all but redundant, I was given the chance to lead. The ethos of the camp was based in a culture of innovation. Yes, there was structure but they trusted me and enabled me to take opportunities. I discovered a Christian faith not to be branded as boring and irrelevant but which seized my dreams.

Too often we are so afraid of what might go wrong we fail to release the potential in our churches. This lack of opportunity for Kris in his journey to adulthood meant he left Christianity. He wasn't able to find his identity, his confidence or an adventure in his church context. As we move from our early teens to adulthood we go through vast changes with significant choices to make. In adolescence you begin dating, start your first job, choose a career and take responsibility. The world offers so much and yet often in our Christian culture we have become too safe. We fail to give our young people responsibility and also allow them to dream for God.

The Jewish tradition sees the importance of this journey to adulthood. The Bar Mitzvah (meaning 'Son of the Commandments') or the Bat Mitzvah (meaning 'Daughter of the Commandments') ceremony marks a coming of age for a boy or girl at the age of thirteen (traditionally the start of puberty). At this ceremony they become responsible for all of their actions and are able to take part in all areas of Jewish life. They can own property, get married and must follow the 613 laws found in the Torah. This Bar Mitzvah tradition is not biblical but appears in Jewish writings from the first century AD. And to this day, it remains a key part of Judaic culture.

This idea of punctuating a journey into adulthood is missing from the Christian church today. Our young people are expected to sit quietly in our meetings rather than their development being publicly acknowledged. Imagine what could happen if we truly empowered our young people to become equal members of our Christian communities. As Jesus left the gospel in the hands of a rabble of disciples, who were probably mostly teenagers too, we also must take calculated risks.

Too late?

Kris's story does not end on a continual search for fantastic powder snow and a yearning for cover shots on ski magazines. At twenty-three, he re-committed his life to Jesus and he now helps lead a surf church based in an old Methodist Chapel overlooking Polzeath beach.

His journey back to faith was perhaps even more dramatic than his leaving. 'I came back to faith over a period of time. The whole coming back to faith was very unchurchy. There was no altar call or preacher initially, just lots of moments, but no believer's prayer.'

So how did you rediscover your faith?

Kris smiled and began to share some of his God moments with me. His parents gave him a white cross from Iona that he put around his neck as he left for a ski season. Another significant thing for him was being in the mountains looking at a photo of his girlfriend. They'd had a sketchy relationship up until that point, but Kris realized she loved him despite everything. He described how love came into his heart and he started to weep.

'I'm sure that was God and the way he was revealing love to me, showing me what love was.'

Yet Kris's story of returning to Jesus went up a gear when he broke his back on Christmas Eve. After being patched up in France, he lived with his parents for two years. He was put in a full body cast for six months then a brace with metal spokes. He thought his life was over as skiing was his life. A month earlier he'd received sponsorship: he'd felt like this was the best life could get and, in an instant, it was all taken away.

Suddenly, he felt like nothing. 'For several months I was suicidal. For ages I just played computer games. That was my life. I eventually began teaching PE, even though my back was still wrecked, in a school with children with learning difficulties. I discovered I had lost who I really was and I had become who others wanted me to be.'

Kris told me how spending time with the kids at school was humbling. Every morning a different minister would come to speak. One time a scouser came to talk on healing. Kris was so sure the man was telling the truth he chatted with him afterwards. This caused Kris to start going to church again.

One ordinary day his back got so bad he had to go home. His parents' vicar rang saying he was coming round to pray, along with a guy called Reg who supposedly had the gift of healing. Kris was rolling a spliff at the time, so he objected forcefully but the minister was determined.

The men came over and asked Kris if he believed in God, and whether he had any faith. The vicar read a passage from James. Reg was stuttering badly, but told Kris a story about his wife's neck being healed. Both men then prayed and Kris felt a sense of peace.

The older man told Kris God was going to heal his back, but there were issues in his life he needed to resolve. They left.

'I then cried for two hours until I couldn't cry anymore.'

When his girlfriend Ness came back, Kris told her he was going to be a Christian, and that she was too! Ness panicked, and the next morning both of them tried to run away by driving to Cornwall in a campervan, thinking they were being brainwashed. Kris had to lie down all the way because his back was so painful.

So you weren't healed? I questioned, intrigued by the twists and turns.

Kris wasn't healed straightaway. He lived in a caravan for the summer with Ness before they decided to move to Newquay, a town popular with tourists. Throughout this time Kris was still reading the Bible every day, despite simultaneously smoking vast quantities of pot.

Surgeons told Kris his back badly needed a major operation. As he left the hospital appointment, Kris found himself wanting to attend a church service – he chose Newquay's Christian Centre as something about the look of it appealed to him. The pastor there told him he needed to trust God to use surgeons to heal his back, or he needed to believe God was going to perform a miracle. When this pastor prayed, Kris knew he needed to stop smoking cannabis – and also get married.

He threw the drugs away on his way to see Ness. He moved out of her flat – three months later they were married.

Kris noticed his back stopped hurting shortly after he made these decisions. 'God had to sort a bunch of stuff out in both Ness's and my life . . . there were lots of tears but God has changed us and we are both now passionate for him.'

Kris's story should give us hope. His passion for adventure is very much alive and active as he takes on the challenges of leading an innovative expression of church amongst the surfing community.

Although people leave God, God does not leave them: 'Here I am! I stand at the door and knock. If anyone hears my voice and opens the door, I will come in and eat with him, and he with me' (Rev. 3:20).

It is tempting to stress the miraculous here. Kris's healing was an instrumental moment in the story. We need to offer to pray for the sick more regularly, daring to risk looking foolish. Yet this story also speaks of the power of relationships with parents, pastors, friends, and with complete strangers. These relationships demonstrated love, not only in the things said but also in the time invested. Kris's re-commitment was not about a single moment at a Christian meeting but about many significant moments. It would have been easy to have given up and missed what God was doing.

These relationships also had authenticity. The people who were speaking into Kris's life were living out their faith. They were not concerned first and foremost with structure, or insisting Kris come to certain meetings, but they met him in his own situation, at the right time. When someone we know loses their faith, we can be so desperate for them to reconnect with God we rush things and pressure them. It took Kris's skiing accident to bring him to a point where he felt he had lost everything. His pride had to be humbled.

So let's live out this adventure together. Let's keep representing Christ's values. Let's be patient but ever-ready. Let's be cool as we discover more of who we are in him.

Practical tips

- Demonstrate God's love, not just through your words, but through your life. Support your friends where you can.
- Realize sometimes people come back to faith immediately but at other times it is a lengthy process.
- Pray God would also use other people to direct your friend, relative or colleague back to him.

4

Pushing Cheesecake

Absolutely nothing could have prepared me for the two-hour conversation about to begin.

Stephen had come straight from work in the City. He was in his early thirties and shook my hand with a firm grip. I noticed how his expensive suit flattered his small frame while he poured us both a glass of wine. We were hidden away in a booth in the corner of swanky bar in central London.

Stephen smiled as he recounted how he grew up in a Christian household, but how Christianity was never forced upon him. His parents became Christians just prior to the birth of Stephen and his twin brother. Their conversion was dramatic and completely changed their lives.

For Stephen growing up, Christianity was simply part of the family's daily life. It wasn't just a Sunday morning thing and they often went away on Christian camps in the holidays.

Stephen was about twelve when he was given the choice to go to church every other week instead of every week. At first he and his brother and sister took advantage of this opportunity, but then they felt like they were missing out and chose to attend weekly again.

I sipped my wine, enjoying the crisp Sauvignon Blanc. 'So was there a point in your childhood where you encountered God?'

Stephen recalls his first significant God moment as when he was six years old at Bible camp. He felt he was having an experience of God and went forward at a meeting, taking the conscious decision to know Jesus. He grinned as he remembered.

His face changed as he told me about school. School wasn't good. Stephen started to hate it when he was quite young and at eleven years old found himself alienated. He was mature for his age and loved being in the presence of adults. The twins were bullied at school, but Stephen, unlike his brother, used to take it to heart. The pair were both thin and short and fairly effeminate looking. His parents weren't great at getting his hair cut and he used to get mistaken for a girl. There were homosexual jokes made about him which he didn't really understand, but he knew he was different. It was then problems began in his relationship with his father.

Stephen took off his suit jacket and placed it neatly on the lime green couch, making himself comfortable as he waited for the next question.

'What kind of problems did you have with your father?'

'Dad didn't affirm me at all. He hadn't been shown affirmation and was a product of his own background. He got on well with my brother, but me and my brother were incredibly different. I found Dad quite emotionless. He didn't seem to care about me, so I made the decision not to care about me. This was about the same time I was having trouble at school.'

Stephen knew he was different but this knowledge actually fortified his personal relationship with God. He was constantly surrounded by things sustaining his faith

– such as Bible verses – and his mum played an important role in his spiritual journey too.

Yet as Stephen developed into a teenager he began to hate himself. He started to have homosexual feelings. 'I cursed myself as I felt there was something wrong with me. I thought if I despised myself enough these feelings would go away.'

His words filled me with sadness. Surprised by his honesty, I asked if the church helped him survive any of this. No.

When Stephen reached his early teens, he joined the youth group and enjoyed going to meetings, but the talks were all about masturbation, sex before marriage and sexuality. Most of these talks were presented in an accusational style and the youth workers pinned together the three issues as if they were 'curses'. Stephen couldn't recall any talks on justice, the poor, charity and grace, and the youth group monthly talks compounded his self-hatred.

I leant back on the foam cushions that were fastened to the wall.

Stephen told a girl about three years older than him he thought he might be gay. She encouraged Stephen to tell one of the youth workers. So after plucking up the courage (despite being terrified that his mother, who was a church leader, might find out) Stephen told one of the leaders.

The youth leader said to Stephen it was a phase he was going through and it would be fine. At the next meeting, he realized the leader had told the other youth workers. That same evening all the youth were asked to stand up if they'd had sex before marriage, masturbated or were struggling with their sexuality. 'It was like ritual humiliation,' Stephen remembers.

'I was surrounded by my peers . . . cool people, people I aspired to be like, my brother and sister . . . All of those people in one room and they asked us to stand up? I was so angry because I knew they wanted to humiliate me. I was going bright red and burning up and everyone was staring at me. I was in absolute terror. I thought, "How could they do that to me?" I was so exposed and terrified. It felt similar to the name calling at school.'

I was shocked by Stephen's account.

He then described how his relationship with God became more and more personal. God was the only person he felt he could trust. Stephen's issue was with church: 'I felt I was rejected, over and over again.'

This was compounded when Stephen chose to have some counselling sessions with a woman at church. He confided in her about his sexuality issues. But on the third session he was a bit late and found one of the church elders sat in the counselling room. The woman told Stephen she had brought him in as she felt it was appropriate and hoped Stephen didn't mind. The fact she hadn't asked his permission meant fourteen-year-old Stephen again felt betrayed. He stopped going to counselling, terrified his mother was going to find out he might be gay.

After another sip of wine Stephen told me he went to church until he was about fifteen. Church got too spiritual and judgemental. He was sorry he couldn't support his mother in her new role as an elder. Although Stephen appeared to be a confident young man, he was in fact completely paranoid.

'I didn't have a relationship with a guy until I was sixteen . . . I was on a release from work to college and I met a gay man who introduced me to a load of other gay people. One night, one of them, who was in his late thirties, was dropping me home and he said, "Can I kiss you?" Now no-one had asked me that before and I started seeing him. My parents didn't know any of this. It was like two worlds existing next to each other.'

'Whilst I was quite excited by it, nothing fully sexual happened. I guess I saw him as an intimate male figure, which was really unusual as my father hadn't been that. It soon got a bit too intense, he was twenty years older than me and so I dropped him. So that was nothing and then when I was eighteen, this dreadful thing happened.'

I met Stephen's gaze, wondering if he could see the rapt attention in mine.

On Stephen's eighteenth birthday he went on holiday. 'And I was raped by another man who was staying in the same apartment block. My parents didn't know about it. My mum was cooking a meal and I went for a walk. It was a safe place. And there was a guy there who had been watching me in the pool earlier in the day. He put something over my mouth and did what he did and then disappeared. The next thing I know I'm standing with my shorts off and my T-shirt all torn.'

'So I pulled the shreds of clothing back on, and walked straight back to the apartment and straight through to the bathroom. I was a bit of a mess and bleeding quite badly. I started brushing my tongue and scrubbing myself in the shower and being sick . . . all those things you do to desperately try and get clean. After that I just lay in bed with a fever. My parents were really worried about me. It was the psychological effect of what had happened. It really messed me up. Two days later and I'd still not been out. The last day before we had to go home, my mum convinced me to go out and when I came out of the block, the man was there, which really messed me up even more. I was sick everywhere, it was horrific but I wouldn't tell my parents what had happened. I was scared it would be my fault in some way, or that I'd be tarnished in some way. I couldn't tell them.'

I nodded tentatively, unsure what to ask next.

Stephen continued, 'We got home and I was still a mess. I couldn't do anything. I didn't want to go out on my own or anything. I ended up with an overwhelming hatred of men and I took it all out on my dad. I was so angry and erratic. We fought so much that eventually, Mum told me I couldn't stay at home as we all needed some space. She found me a counsellor and I moved in with him and his family for a few weeks.'

There was a moment of silence. As I realized the intensity of what Stephen had just shared, we both looked away, focusing instead on the huge fish tank at the end of our booth. The exotic fish shimmered in the light.

'How was your relationship with God through all of this?'

Stephen remembers screaming out to God – falling on his knees and begging him to rescue him.

'The counsellor was great and eventually I forgave my dad.' He hesitated. 'The counsellor encouraged me to tell my mum about my sexuality. He said, "She won't reject you or be angry," but I wasn't sure. Eventually I agreed. I was aware that once I'd said it, I couldn't un-say it. So I took her for a walk and told her, "I think I'm gay." She started crying. It really hurt me, I thought she would but it really did hurt. But within a minute, she said, "Look, you're my son, I love you and always will and that's all that matters. It's not what I'd choose but I love you and will love you no matter what." This was exactly the right thing to say, and then she cried, and the more she cried the more I cried. So we went to a coffee shop, hugged and pushed cheesecake around a plate with a fork, unsure of what to say. But at that moment, she became my best friend really.'

Stephen put off telling his father. His life took many more twists and turns, as he struggled with sickness, depression and alcohol dependency. He lived in Greece and worked for a Christian holiday company, and was again damaged by the church.

'When I got back from Greece, Mum said, "I really think you should tell your dad." I was twenty-six by this point. I had my backpack ready to leave for London as I was sure that as soon as I told him I was gay, he'd kick me out. He was sat in the lounge and I said, "I've got something to tell you." Once I had told him, he responded, "Look, Stephen, I don't have a problem with homosexuality." I hadn't expected this reaction and I glimpsed something of Jesus in his attitude.'

Stephen was amazed by how great his dad had been at this time, demonstrating more about Christianity than ever before.

Stephen later left for London and moved in with his partner.

As I began to wrap up the interview, Stephen said 'I hate living a lonely life with Christ. I don't want to expose myself to the church and so I am gay and alone.'

His words made me want to weep.

Flesh and blood

It's extremely easy to have views on an issue before it becomes flesh and blood.

I remember as a young person being told in my youth group that homosexuality was wrong. Young people would often call each other 'gay' as a juvenile insult. Homosexuality was always spoken about as a theological issue not as an everyday reality. In a very real way there was almost a sense of fear of the organized rainbow-flag-waving gay community.

It wasn't until I was sixteen I was confronted with the reality of same-sex relationships. I was working in a menswear department and suddenly working and socializing with gay men. I discovered they were not to be feared but were actually normal people.

Listening to Stephen's story reminded me why the church often has a bad name – our theology is often built in an academic cocoon rather than in relationships. It's not difficult to have homophobic views until you discover someone close to you is gay. It's also not difficult to lump together sexual sins in a theology book – but I can understand Stephen's frustration when masturbation, sex before marriage and homosexuality were continually listed in the same sentence.

Yes, they are all about sex but they have extremely different implications. Masturbation is about issues of lust. Sex before marriage is different. It is not just about an inability to wait, but it has an impact on another. Homosexuality is different again. It's about your entire sexual orientation: a key part of a person's identity. To refrain from homosexuality is about relinquishing dreams of a lifelong partner and children, and being unable to fit nicely into church culture. It is huge.

I help edit a Christian youth magazine and a year ago we led with an article about homosexuality. I was amazed by the number of emails we had from people struggling with their sexuality. They were not just young people but youth workers and church leaders too. They were grappling in secret with it, afraid that if they were to share their real selves with others in the church, then they would be condemned.

The issue is taboo and it was heart-breaking to hear Stephen's internal struggles he could not talk through. Confusion, self-hate and anger are volatile emotions. Hiding the rape incident from his family demonstrates the extent of his shame about his sexuality.

We have inadvertently created a fear in our churches of being open about sexuality. Homosexuality was over-simplified to Stephen. A single prayer would re-orient you, or it was just seen as a phase.

God can answer a simple prayer but it would be naïve to think this is always the case. And homosexuality may be a phase for a few but when we belittle such a massive confession in this way we are failing to give the individual space to explore further.

Homosexuality is growing in visibility in our culture. It is now taught in our schools as normal. The media portrays it as a valid lifestyle choice. Many Christians ignore the issue because we just do not know how to respond.

Homosexuality divides families, churches and denominations. We have elevated it to centre stage, making it a super sin. Why has it been given this status? Core doctrine covers elements such as the Trinity, the character of God, and the power of the cross. Homosexuality is not there but it is often treated as if it was. Why?

Phyllis Tickle answers this by pointing out the Protestant Church is built on the foundation of 'Scriptura sola' – that all authority in Christianity is based on Scripture alone. However, over the last century this premise has been undermined time and time again. We had views on slavery, gender equality, divorce and female ordination based on the Bible alone that have been reformed (for the vast majority of Christendom). Tickle argues, 'Of all the fights, the gay one must be – has to be – the bitterest, because once it is lost, there are no more fights to be had. It is finished. Where now is the authority?'[16] She states if the church changes its standpoint, then we will need to redefine where our authority comes from.

Whatever your take on Tickle's argument, homosexuality should never have been given such prominence. In the Gospel accounts, Jesus never spoke about same-sex relationships. Some theologians argue homosexuality was just not an issue of the day amongst the Jewish people but Jesus did speak about lust and about divorce. Yet his biggest gripe was against religious 'know-it-alls' who showed no grace: people who pointed out the splinter in someone else's eye but failed to see the branch in their own. The church has become notorious for its lack of grace about homosexuality. Grace is not about condoning, but loving.

Ultimately, the discussion comes down to whether practising homosexuals are fully accepted by God. And this gets to the core of our faith, asking the difficult question: how inclusive is God's love?

Andrew Marin, with his book *Love is an Orientation*, is helping to build a bridge between the gay community and the church by elevating the conversation on sexuality and faith. Whilst being a conservative evangelical, he has moved to a predominantly gay neighbourhood so he can understand the issues: 'Believers are convinced they know what gays and lesbians think, but actually GLBT [Gay, Lesbian, Bisexual and Transgender] people's real thoughts and fears are totally different.'

He goes on to unpack some of the key questions the gay community is asking the church. Questions like, Will Christians always look at me as just gay? Do Christians believe I chose to be like this? Do Christians think I am going to proposition them or abuse their children? When will the church reject me or kick me out?

It's time we took the power out of this topic. By creating a real openness in our churches to talk about sexuality, we could rob it of the destructiveness secretly eating away at people. Stephen told me the guy who had counselled him had in fact been gay himself but had chosen not to tell Stephen at that time. Stephen's frustration was evident, 'I had no-one to talk to. Why didn't people who had been through similar things talk about it? Why didn't they help me believe I could get through this? Why did they feel they had to hide it? There were people who could have helped me but it was almost as if they were too scared to talk about it for fear of rejection.'

But where do you stand?

I dread those moments.

You are sharing something of your faith journey. Your good friend is asking searching questions about God. The conversation is flowing well and then they ask that question, 'So what's your view on homosexuality?'

See, I am embarrassed about how wrong we, the church, have got it in the past. We have justified all kinds of horrendous actions from the Crusades to slavery and now we try and justify our homophobia. I don't want my generation to tarnish the church with a bad name again.

Our society publicly and persuasively affirms the validity of same-sex relationships. There is an understanding in our culture that there is no right or wrong sexuality, we must all accept the lifestyles of others. With such strong public opinion, it's extremely controversial to hold a different viewpoint.

So we use phrases like, 'Love the sinner hate the sin.'

It seems to make sense. We love the individual but despise the behaviour failing to reach God's standards. I can love someone in the local pub but hate the sinful way they gossip. I can love someone in my church but hate their sinful love of money. So it would make sense I could love someone who is gay and hate their sinful sexual exploits.

But here is the crux of the issue. The gay community are a community because they have rallied around what makes them different. Their sexual behaviour is what sets them apart from everyone else. We want to neatly say that behaviour is separate from our identity but, unsurprisingly, when you tell a gay person you love them but hate their behaviour, it is not warmly received. Who they are and what they do is intricately related: behaviour is identity.[17]

So let's look at the biblical basis for this view. Most of the argument is based around six key texts (Lev. 18:22, Lev. 20:13, Deut. 23:17–18, Rom. 1:26–27, 1 Cor. 6:9 and 1 Tim. 1:9–10). Each text has been debated intensively. There are arguments about the context of these writings, the original audience for them and about whether the writers are speaking of promiscuous same-sex encounters or committed same-sex relationships.

All six texts speak only about sexual behaviour rather than orientation. This has been one of the elements underlying the sexuality debate.

When we begin to look at orientation the argument spills into nature versus nurture. If people are born with genes that give them homosexual attraction, then some would surmise this is the way God intended them to be – but if the attraction is a result of conditioning then others would argue people should simply change their behaviour.

That argument could well go on for eternity. It is impossible to prove one way or another. We then come back to Scripture and its interpretation. We should not hold an opinion just because someone has told us what to believe. We must own our faith, sifting through the arguments of both sides rather than taking someone else's viewpoint.

For awkward theological issues that impact so many, it is easy to sit on the fence. However, if we are truly going to help people with homosexual feelings move forward in their relationship with Jesus, then we need to humbly come to some conclusion ourselves.

So, having wrestled with the key verses and the bigger biblical narrative, I don't think 'being gay' is sinful. However, I do think same-sex sexual relationships are not God's best for our lives. I believe same-sex sexual relationships fall short of what God calls us to: they are as sinful as sleeping with someone outside of wedlock.

Now, I understand what I have said will be offensive to many. I sometimes wish the Christian faith was less offensive. I sometimes wish people could just say a prayer and get on with their lives, doing whatever seems best in their own eyes. But as we come to Jesus, as we choose to put our faith in him, he wants us to be transformed.

We must get beyond our trite phrases and begin to separate behaviour from identity. There is truth in 'love the sinner, hate the sin' but it's more complex than that.

The formation of identity is highly important. Christianity is about finding our true identity not in our career, possessions or sexual partner; but in Christ. This can be painful. If our identity comes from our image, we must let this die. We must instead embrace our new identity in our relationship with Jesus.

This is a challenge for all. In my early twenties I one day realized I was defining my identity more in my role than in my relationship with Jesus. I still wrestle to know I am loved by God for who I am rather than what I do.

For people like Stephen, this may potentially be much harder. I would expect that some members of the gay community have based their identity on their sexuality as they have fought prejudice as a societal minority. In many ways, when we are a minority in society, our difference arguably begins to define our identity to a much greater extent. In Stephen's case, his sexuality had become the basis of his identity.

We have failed to understand perspectives within the gay community. We study and educate ourselves on different cultural world views but have we ever educated ourselves on the values, the questions and the lifestyle choices that form a framework for gay people? Have we ever explored how gay individuals define their identity?

The problem is we often talk about the sexuality issue in a vacuum. The issue needs to be made personal: we must not limit our friendships to those of the same sexual orientation as us. We must stop seeing each gay person as a threat or as 'an issue' and instead see them, like us, as individuals searching for love. We must see each person from God's perspective, no matter what their sexual preference.

Sometimes we play God. We judge and convict but we are not called to be judge and convictor. We easily point the finger but we all have areas of our lives that displease God. All Christians are recovering sinners. The Holy Spirit convicts and one day each of us will appear before the throne of God and be judged.

Our role is to love.

I cannot imagine what it must have been like for Stephen to go through his teenage years with no support as he tried to follow Jesus whilst trying to understand his sexuality. I am not sure where I would be had I been gay and experienced the same treatment. But I want to stand alongside others in Stephen's situation and show them Christ's love.

If only Jesus was here

Jesus always knew what to do. No matter what scenario unfolded before him, he always had the right response.

Unfortunately, we are not Jesus and we often just do not know what to do.

Jennifer Ashley writes about this dilemma with honesty. She says,

> What is your call, then, as a Christian, as a follower of Christ, as someone who has the grace of the Lord in their life, when your friend is gay? What do you say? What do you do? What does it mean to love them like Jesus would? You wonder, gazing into the back of your eyelids at night, if this is even possible within the limits of our human capacity to love?[18]

The sexuality issue is not going to go away. We can't just bury our heads in the sand.

Jesus saw beyond the tax collector, the adulterer and the fisherman. The gay community Andrew Marin works with thank him for his Bible studies because he 'treat[s] us like children of God and not gays and lesbians who want to be Christians'.[19]

Jesus ate and socialized with those who would not have been welcome in the synagogue. The Pharisees criticized Jesus for the company he kept but when was the last time we were criticized for the company we keep?

Jesus answered closed questions with bigger kingdom questions. He was able to change the whole direction of a conversation. How can we widen the debate on sexuality to focus more on our new identity in Christ?

Jesus protected the woman caught in adultery from the religious mob ready to stone her to death. We should be helping to protect people like Stephen from the hatred that still exists in pockets of our church and society.

We need to be more like Jesus. But this is not easy.

As the interview closed, I asked Stephen, if he could speak to a thousand church clergy now, what he would say.

His words were like daggers of conviction: 'Learn about compassion. Learn about grace. Be sensitive. Pointing the finger is not going to help gay people understand who they are, what they are and what they should be doing. Church should be a supportive community that honours God and honours each other.'

The church has made some mistakes: we have been far too reactionary, afraid, judgemental and unloving. In the brilliant book *Blue Like Jazz*, Donald Miller recounts the story of setting up a confession booth on his university campus. It is a crazy idea but students on the notoriously unchristian campus line up to go to confession. The twist is that as each person enters the booth, they do not confess their sins but Miller confesses the sins of the church and asks for their forgiveness.

There is something profound and beautiful about that image. If we are ever going to see people like Stephen re-connect with Jesus and the church, we must begin by saying sorry: sorry for failing to learn about compassion; sorry for failing to remember grace; sorry for failing to honour every person who is created in the image of God.

There will be many questions ahead as we begin to welcome gay people into our church community so they meet with Jesus. There will be tricky conversations to be had and tough issues to overcome. I know I do not have all the answers and I have only just begun to struggle with the complexity of identity, sexuality and faith. We may never have all the answers but as Jesus spent time with the Father, so must we, as we learn how to be children of God.

Empty

The wine bottle was now empty. The fish were still shimmering.

'So is there anything about church you miss?'

'Yes, the worship,' Stephen said, without even a second to reflect. 'I worship on my own, but I miss the corporate worship.' He recounted various worship experiences from his childhood that had been mountain-top moments of engaging with God. 'I miss teaching. I miss hearing about Jesus and life and God.'

'I feel I have a relationship with God, not with church. He understands me . . . he talks to me . . . he lifts me . . . he loves me . . . he's been consistent throughout. I've left him a number of times, but he's never left me.' He paused. 'For me, homosexuality is an issue. I don't like it, I don't accept it, and that's part of the church heritage. I've not moved on and I have never really been happy. I don't believe this is what God wants for me, but I don't see a way out. And I tried. I have a great job, am quite wealthy, but feel a bit shit about my life really.'

Our meeting left me numb. Stephen's raw honesty was painful to hear. He had managed to maintain his faith in God despite the church, rather than because of the church. As I wandered back through the streets of London that evening, again I wanted to cry. *This is no longer an issue, this is flesh and blood.*

Practical tips

- Spend time listening, trying to understand your friend's perspective.
- It may be appropriate to apologize for judgemental views you have harboured or to acknowledge times when the church has failed to demonstrate love.
- Help your friend focus on their relationship with God before focusing on lifestyle issues. Allow God to convict.

5

The Anti-Epiphany

It was a hot day on the South Bank. I had met Jo minutes earlier at Waterloo station. Jo is a mature student in her mid twenties. Her striking facial features were framed by the red and white keffiyeh around her neck and she wore fashionable white-framed glasses.

The café we had chosen is known for its exceptional hot chocolate. So, despite the weather, we ordered two massive hot chocolates. We found some seats in the shade of an umbrella, our drinks separating us on the small unstable table. Jo was just five foot tall but burst into conversation with the energy of a giant, 'So you want to know about my family background first?'

I nodded, wiping my mouth of chocolaty froth.

Jo launched into her story. Her father was in the services and so the family moved around a lot. She lived in Northern Ireland in the eighties, then Bristol and then London. Her father came from a Catholic background but when she was young he became an evangelical Christian.

'He was in the RAF and was an engineer. The RAF and his upbringing were very hierarchical. Also I was really ashamed of what he did . . . of the way he acted at home . . . and the fact his job was so imperialistic and ultimately about killing people . . . it wasn't something to be proud of.'

Her anti-institutional opinions were indicated by her lip piercing and the tattoos that marked her wrist. She explained how her mother hadn't become a Christian until Jo was seventeen. There was always tension in the house about Christianity and her father took being the head of the household to an extreme. Whatever he said was completely correct and couldn't be argued with and the fact that her mother wasn't a Christian, meant her views weren't considered important at all.

'So what happened for your mum to become a Christian? Was she worn down after 17 years?' I joked.

'Quite possibly,' Jo said.

Her frustration was evident as she shared about the difficulties of moving around the country, of a father who was often away, of having nowhere to call home.

Jo went to a Christian school with which she also struggled. She found it failed to represent the values of Jesus, being based instead on the class system. She also disliked church because she found it irrelevant.

Jo nursed the large hot chocolate with hands dwarfed by its enormity. The gentle cloud of steam rose from the cup as she expanded on her comments. She spoke about the troubles she had faced, such as her eating disorder and how the church's teaching never spoke to her situation.

I was bewildered as to how she ever became a Christian.

Her glossy brown hair brushed her shoulders as she spoke. She made a commitment to Jesus when she was fourteen. She had a secret spiritual longing and, at the time, she was going through a tough period; she had a lot of problems. 'Becoming a Christian was a balm – faith help reassure me. I loved lots of the Old Testament stuff, like the Psalms. So at fifteen I got baptized.'

Her eyes focused on the frothy top of the half empty hot chocolate. She felt Christianity had value but, for her, it was very much about her personal experience rather than the Christian culture. She had outgrown her local church where there seemed no passion for anything. The church wasn't spiritual or outward-looking; it seemed to be just about coffee mornings. And so, she moved churches. She wanted to be with the adults, not sectioned off with the youth.

'But I found my new church difficult too. I did a preaching course, an evening a week, but at the end of it, I was the only one who wasn't allowed to preach. I was never told why and I felt rubbish.'

Despite her issues with church, Jo's faith was still exceptionally active. She frowned as she recounted how she read her Bible intensively – spending more time doing that than studying. She believed discipleship meant living simply, had cut out lots of good elements of her life and was tithing about half her wage from her Saturday job.

'Do you think you were too hard on yourself?' I asked.

'Well, it depends how you interpret what Jesus says.' Her challenging tone was convincing. 'If you're really called to walk with him, then we have to listen to the things he says. We have such a cushy life, especially materially. I wanted to walk with him completely – I felt called to impact the nations – so everything that wasn't of him had to go.'

After school she moved to south London for her gap year. Here she found a truly special church situation. She loved the real community, the lack of hierarchy, the vulnerability, the informality, the genuineness. 'It's just a real shame that some of the people who made it that way are now dead, which I really struggle with.'[20]

With another sip of hot chocolate, she said, 'And my spiritual walk blossomed in that time. That church community did a lot of good. If I died, I'd want to have my funeral there . . .'

However, as the gap year came to an end, Jo lost her faith. A few weeks before helping to host a big mission she suddenly stopped believing in Jesus. The loss of faith was almost like an anti-epiphany: it all fell apart. As she was reading through the gospels, she thought, 'Did this God that I've had all these experiences with really come to earth as Jesus? Did he really walk on the earth and do this, this and this?' In a moment, it just stopped making sense for her. She no longer believed it could all be completely true.

I nodded, trying to understand her perspective.

'I come from a culture, the evangelical Christian culture, where you read something and accept it. And that's ingrained in you. You believe it's true because it was written down a long time ago and there is historical verification. However tenuous the links are, you still have this thing in your mind and your spirit that says, "This is correct." It is so ingrained. That's why I find it hard talking to you about this.'

Jo had had issues with Scripture before. When she was fourteen there had been an awkward situation when one of the older guys in the youth group had done some inappropriate things and abused other girls in the group. The abuse meant Jo questioned her sexuality and at that young age, she believed she was gay.

She had a liberal view of homosexuality and just holding this viewpoint made her feel sinful, as she felt she was failing to take the Word of God seriously. She thought if she wanted to walk with Jesus, she had to have a certain view of the Bible.

Intrigued by the fact that someone had lost their faith by reading Scripture, I asked her to explain again the moment of losing faith.

She collected her thoughts. 'I just thought, everything I am doing in dying to myself relies on the person of Jesus being absolutely true and if it's not then everything instantly falls apart. That was a shit moment.'

'And so this was a moment, not a gradual process?' I was transfixed and listened intently to every word.

'It was a moment, an absolute moment.'

Five minutes after her anti-epiphany, a friend called her mobile saying, 'God's told me you're upset.' Her response was to say, 'No, I don't believe in God. I'm not a Christian anymore.'

'I just knew that the story of Jesus was not true. That the claims the Bible made just were not accurate.'

As the anti-epiphany struck, Jo's life's foundations were eroded. She smiled bravely as she said, 'Suddenly everything fell apart. When I told people, some of them reacted as if someone had died. They burst into tears. It was really hard. I didn't have any money or a home, and I pretty much had a nervous breakdown. I had felt called to south London, I had felt that I had a duty and yet the fundamental belief system that had supported all these things was suddenly gone.'

She ate a spoonful of the froth from the bottom of the mug. 'So I was trying to work out, is there a God? Do I go to church? How do I meet my needs? Do I pray? My whole life had been so focused on God I could not look at anything objectively.'

Jo's Christian friends reacted in different ways but all of them were scared by her confession. If Jo could lose her faith, then could they?

She explained, 'See, I didn't backslide, it wasn't like I wanted to sin. I know people who really love Jesus, yet they get completely drunk every weekend and they can't marry their lifestyle with their faith. I also know people who are really angry with God. But I wasn't either of these. My decision came from a really rational decision that my interpretation of the Bible was wrong. From there everything fell apart.'

Bringing her thoughts to a conclusion she continued, 'So there are three reasons why I don't believe: firstly because of the colonizing, patriarchal practices of the church, people are often motivated to evangelize for a whole host of wrong reasons. Secondly, I just can't believe that Jesus is the son of God – he was definitely a spiritual man but the idea that he was also full God just doesn't add up – Jesus is so different to the God of the Old Testament. The Bible is so vague about so much – about heaven and hell – even the resurrection – there are so many different accounts, so what happened? How can we be sure it happened the way it says it did? And then, thirdly, there is the whole idea of God itself. I couldn't articulate who this God was.'

Having lost her entire paradigm, Jo needed to reconnect with something so at this time she went to Catholic Mass. With her evangelical head, she didn't feel right to be in a Catholic church and she would argue with the priest. But Mass provided her with something ritualistic. 'It was almost as if I knew the sociology of religion and I wanted to fake things just to cope. I even got confirmed. See, being a Catholic seemed easier than being an evangelical Christian.'

'You spoke earlier about prophesying and so on: how do you explain all of that now?' I asked.

'There were a lot of things I could now explain away. The way I rationalize these things makes me look like an idiot. Like, I'd been speaking in tongues since the age of sixteen, I'd seen demons, I'd heard angels, I'd prophesied

stuff, I'd felt God saying, "Do x, y and z and this will happen," and when I obeyed, those things happened.'

She went on to argue there are powerful stimuli that
impact our brain. Apparently, we interpret these stimuli
as spirituality and this makes experiences seem real. 'I
am now not sure whether those things were as I experienced them or whether I just attributed them to a belief
system that was so ingrained and so powerful.'

I left the interview with Jo exhausted. I often hear stories of people coming to faith as they read the Bible but I
had never come across a Christian who lost their faith
from reading the Bible.

On the surface it all seemed to be going so 'right'. Jo was
preaching at youth events, prophesying, praying, attending church, reading the Bible – how could this happen?

Unanswered questions?

Although there appears to have been a moment in Jo's
story, it is clear there had been lots of underlying issues
and a whole series of questions had already begun to
undermine her bedrock of faith.

Lots of research has been done into patterns of faith
and belief and as I mulled over Jo's faith journey, I found
these models of faith helpful in understanding what
happened.

James Fowler is one of the leading theorists on faith
journeys and his 'stages of faith' model is used widely.[21]
The premise for his work is that faith is not static but
continually evolving. Fowler argues that faith should be
a verb rather than noun. The focus is, therefore, not on
'what' we believe but how we believe.

Alan Jamieson uses Fowler's model in his book
Churchless Faith. He argues it is an extremely helpful way

of understanding faith although the faith stage map gives very broad brushstrokes and is certainly not authoritative.[22]

Fowler's six stages of faith (which begin in early childhood) and other social scientists' work on faith have been simplified by Brian McLaren into four stages; I repeat them here in the hope they will help us understand Jo's journey.

Stage 1: Simplicity

In stage one, everything is clear cut. Faith is about believing in the right things. There are no grey areas; everything is either right or wrong, good or bad.

In stage one, faith is built around belonging to the right church with the right theology with the right answers. There is a belief that everything can be known and that faith is about knowing all the answers. In this phase, leaders are seen as all-knowing and sometimes as God-like.

Jo seemed to have entered this stage in her teens, when she first became a Christian. Although she might have felt she did not fit in with her local church, she had said how she loved watching certain TV preachers.

According to McLaren, in this phase people are highly committed but at the same time, they may come across as intolerant with a simplistic faith. Her actions were definitely ones of commitment. I don't know many young people who have such a zest for the Bible and would tithe 40 to 50 per cent of their wages. She also appears to have been critical of the local church which she felt was failing to live out the commissions of Jesus correctly.

As people with a stage one faith journey along, they may become disillusioned with leaders who fall from grace or may come across differences of opinion that

Losing Faith

become grey areas. During this time, faith shifts from a quest for internal knowledge to a quest for external success as they move into stage two. Fowler's theory argues these transitions are not easy but are often major upheavals.

Stage 2: Complexity

In stage two, the focus shifts from being right or wrong to being effective or ineffective. It is about mastering the right techniques in order to reach certain goals. It is characterized by practical action and is about finding the best approach or process to successfully achieve. This phase of faith is normally intertwined with a real enthusiasm but at the same time it can come across as being quite superficial and naïve.

It appears Jo's faith became outward-focused as it developed. She cultivated a prophetic gift and learnt how to preach. She began to lead others to faith and shortly before she lost her faith, she was helping to co-ordinate a large scale mission. Her faith was about being effective.

McLaren argues people leave this phase as they continue to attempt to make sense of what is true and it is often coupled with the personal disillusionment as techniques fail to deliver.

Stage 3: Perplexity

In stage three, the focus shifts again, and this time to being honest or dishonest. The hard facts of reality lead to a wrestling for understanding as everything is thrown into question. Authority figures are seen as controlling, imposing trite answers to the complexity of life.

In this Perplexity stage, people often come across as cynical and uncommitted. McLaren states people in stage three are attempting to discern whether God is a myth, a social construct or a mystery worth seeking.

It is in this stage three Jo had found herself. She was experiencing intense confusion on issues as varied as healing, sexuality and the validity of the Bible.

Her faith had moved out of phase one; things were no longer as clear cut. During the interview, I asked if she thought the Christian faith tried to oversimplify things.

Her response had been illuminating. 'Yeah, it's all oversimplified and yet not understood enough. The whole "Say sorry, ask him into your heart, say thank you, you're saved"; that's so oversimplified. And the whole, "Guys, you don't need to get into theology, it's easy! God loves you and all you need to do is this . . ." It's ridiculous.'

Jo had also moved through phase two. She had prayed for a close friend again and again, as she anointed her with oil. And yet her friend, a committed Christian, died in her early thirties from cancer. Alongside this, although she had seen the miraculous in certain trivial situations, her eyesight has deteriorated since she was seventeen; to the point at which now she is considered disabled. The 'praying with faith for healing' process did not work.

When I asked her what annoyed her, she spoke of how she was always introduced as '"Jo, who used to be a Christian". And time and time again, I'd have the same arguments, and Christians would regurgitate stupid phrases that were based on the premise that the Bible was the Word of God, which I had already refuted.'

Jo entered the Perplexity phase with a host of questions, struggling honestly. And then one day, the 'anti-epiphany' came and she decided Christianity was a myth – Jesus was not really who the Bible claims.

McLaren writes that in stage three you are humbled, whether you keep or lose your faith. Faith is no longer based on authority figures. It is no longer as idealistic. And you must now take responsibility for your own journey.

By rejecting her Christian faith, Jo was humbled. She had to re-evaluate everything: 'life requires one to make commitments, and commitments grow out of values and beliefs, so one is not left with the option of staying in limbo. One has to make choices.'[23]

Stage 4: Humility

In the fourth and final stage, the focus shifts again, from being honest or dishonest to being wise or unwise. The undergirding principal is about reaching one's potential, striving to make a difference in the world. In this stage, faith is based on a few absolute truths, whilst recognising that much remains a mystery.

McLaren calls this stage humility because we understand how little we know. At the same time, the search for understanding, epitomized in stages one and two, continues, as well as the constant questioning found in stage three; but the goal has changed. The goal now is to invest life wisely.

Space

Jo's faith journey seems to fit well with these stages. But McLaren's faith stages can be used unhelpfully. Each stage of faith has both its positives and its negatives. We mustn't value one over another and we mustn't try and push people to a different stage. Not everyone will journey through all four stages.

Generally, the church is excellent at helping people make sense of their faith in stage one and stage two. We are brilliant at giving people the 'right' answers and at helping people become effective in mission, prayer or some other spiritual discipline. The problem is the church is not brilliant at helping people work through questions.

Over the last few years I have been reading the Bible in my local pub with a range of people; some Christians and some who are not. The questions new Christians or not-yet-Christians ask are intriguing. They always pick up on the issues I don't want them to pick up on. They ask questions that challenge the authority of Scripture; query the reality of angels and demons; and oppose many of my perspectives on God. I find these Bible discussions insightful. They are hard but healthy.

At times we can be afraid of the questions that will arise. We prefer a pre-packaged sermon on a Sunday morning, rather than dialogue that allows people to debate. Now, I preach and preaching is important but we must also create space for dialogue, for people to ask those difficult questions. Was Jo given the space to ask questions about sexuality and healing – issues that had begun to undermine her beliefs before her anti-epiphany?

Bob Ekblad reads the Bible with prisoners, immigrants and the poor and documents this in *Reading the Bible with the Damned*. He argues if we just preach, we produce dependency rather than allowing individuals to be free as they develop their understanding.[24] Our faith becomes built upon teaching from the front and fails to be a personal relationship with God.

Like Ekblad, we need to create space to engage with the Bible in the context of everyday life with everyday people. This will create space for questions. And in this space, we need to grant permission to share doubts, struggles and fears.

As I read the Bible in my local pub, I regularly come across questions to which I do not know the answer. I have to simply say I do not know – but the questions set me on a quest for meaning and understanding. We need the boldness to confess our ignorance and a commitment to find out the answers.

The safety net

Although we may help our Christian communities explore how to create space for questioning, it is much harder to know how to re-connect with people like Jo. It is clear she does not want to be barraged with trite answers. She appears very closed to even exploring the Christian faith again – a 'been there, done that' mentality.

I love fixing situations but I can not magically fix someone's faith. This is so frustrating. We can pray. Sure.

But I always want to do something practically.

The most vital thing we can offer Jo is to be there: a safety net of friendship. Friendship that is real and honest, so that whenever she wants to talk about belief again, we can be open to her questions and real about her doubts. Yet until then, and even if 'then' never arrives, we must respect and value each friend, irrespective of where their faith is at: in short, we must simply love them.

A faithless love?

When Jo speaks, her eyes blaze with passion. As the interview drew to a conclusion she talked fervently about her work in Palestine. She helps the Palestinians persecuted under Israeli occupation in the Gaza Strip and the West Bank. As she made sacrifices in her teens to follow Jesus, she is again making costly sacrifices but for a different cause. Her heart yearns for justice.

She contemplated the role her faith played in creating the passion she has for Palestine. 'I still have the values such as justice but I have lost the religion. I took what I could take from Jesus whilst not believing he was the son of God.'

'The fact I love people and value people is really important to me. That for me is spiritual. Now I'm not trying to convert people, I have more time to love people – to be just, to walk humbly, to be merciful . . . When you walk with God, whether God is real or a mental force you create, you strive to be better but when you relax and stop trying to be something you're not, you can enjoy life more.'

We parted ways and I realized how much I love Jo's passion for people and passion for justice. Her life embodies so many worthy values and I can understand many of her problems with Christianity. We can become so focused on our own sin and so desperate to convert people, that we lose track of God's bigger vision.

Becoming better people should come naturally as we begin to know more of Jesus' love. Sharing our faith should not be our ulterior motive for loving others but should flow from the love we have received from him. Perhaps we need to rediscover the kingdom vision of God . . .

And as I took the train journey home, I continued to puzzle over Jo's loss of faith. I hope one day she discovers a stage-four faith in Jesus, she rediscovers a God who loves her and wants his love and grace to overflow from her into this broken world. May she continue to walk humbly and love justice . . . and one day know Jesus again.

Practical tips

- There are times to speak and times to be quiet. We often talk of the Holy Spirit's prompting to talk but we rarely consider the Holy Spirit can ask us to be quiet. Sometimes we need to wait for our friends to bring up issues of belief rather than forcing a situation.
- As people lose faith, their entire worldview changes and this can cause a massive emotional upheaval. They may need our support as they go through this.
- When matters of faith come to the forefront again, it is important to journey alongside as a co-pilgrim.

6

Looming Clouds

'And would you call it backsliding?' I asked.

'No, I think it was part of my growth,' Chris replied.

We had met at an old river boat which was swamped by pot plants. It was low tide and the dirty banks of the River Thames matched the greyness of the clouds looming over the top of us. It was warm, but rain was definitely in the post. We sat out on the battered deck and Chris opened his pasta lunch.

Chris has a way of almost thinking out loud and his artistic flair is evident in the way he communicates. 'My parents are Christian in as much as they are British,' he began. 'Well, that's been my take on it.' His parents had been raised as Christians, his father an altar boy and his mother had been to a church school. 'Certainly as I was growing up, they didn't instil a faith in me but they weren't opposed to it either.'

Chris used to go to church on occasion for midnight mass as a child and had been sent to church schools. Christian culture just seemed to be the norm where he lived on the south coast.

'I was certainly aware of God and Christianity from the age I started going to school – we'd say prayers and sing hymns in school assembly. Sometimes I'd speak about it with my parents, but whenever I did, I'd feel a bit nervous. I don't know why. I guess because it wasn't normal to talk about this stuff at home. Christianity was just part of life.'

As Chris entered adolescence, he became more aware of himself in relation to the world and more aware of spirituality generally. He was always a deep thinker and was fascinated by supernatural things. He used to read books on the paranormal and, at the age of thirteen, he started to think more about his personal spirituality.

Chris began to be interested in religion: 'Buddhism was quite cool and I knew people who were into Wicker.' He had a number of friends who were Christians; in particular, one of his closest friends had a significant influence on him, 'Not because he evangelized but because we hung out,' Chris said.

'Then we went on a school trip to Iona with a couple of Christian teachers. I came away having had some experience of God, I think. When I left, I bought a pin badge cross.'

Being in his mid teens and living in rural Dorset, Chris had the choice of either trying to get into pubs or joining his friend's Christian youth group. He decided to explore Christianity. 'I deliberated about going for a while, but the first time I went, I stepped in the door and this girl came running up to me in a hyperactive fourteen-year-old kind of way and started jumping up and down. We end up seeing each other for about a year and a half.'

Interesting technique, I thought to myself. Chris grinned, his smile infectious.

Because of this girlfriend and other people at the youth group, Chris started going to church. 'I knew that Christians actually liked me and valued me and wanted me in their friendship group,' he mused. 'In contrast to other people at school who I'd been hanging out with . . .'

Chris told of going to Bible study groups and asking annoying questions until, one day, he was invited to a large church event in Bournemouth. Days before the event, his girlfriend explained if she started crying or began hugging him, it would be because of God.

'So I get there and there's a young funky Christian band playing young funky Christian songs and lots of enthusiastic Christians and, shock horror, they're raising their hands in worship. I didn't really know what to make of it. My first impression was one of mild discomfort, which was alleviated by the fact that I was with my new friends.'

Chris got goose-bumps during the worship and a tingling sensation. He was given a four-inch nail to meditate on as a young guy sporting blond dreadlocks, cream combats and a blue Hawaiian shirt gave a gospel presentation. 'I was just sixteen. It was impacting stuff and the first time I heard it like that. I remember going to the front and kneeling down . . .'

From this point on Chris realized God was real. He continued going to an Anglican church but although his beliefs had changed, his lifestyle hadn't. A few years later there came another event and another pivotal moment. 'I got baptized in the Holy Spirit although I didn't know what it was at the time. When this dude prayed for me, I started to speak in tongues. It opened up a whole new level for me. I had belief but then I had experienced the Holy Spirit and what it means to commune with him, it opened everything up and I felt like I was communicating with God in a much more intimate way.'

Chris chuckled as he recollected arriving home. His mother asked if he'd had fun and the first thing Chris said was, 'It was brilliant! I started speaking in tongues!'

'I think my parents thought I had joined a cult,' Chris said.

When Chris went to university he became extremely passionate about evangelism – partly because he felt he should but also because he had a genuine excitement about introducing people to Jesus. Chris invested his energy in the Christian Union, which became his main church community whilst he flitted between two local churches, depending on who was offering a free student lunch.

'Within a year I was invited to join the Executive Committee and I became the evangelism secretary – so evangelism was a big thing for me.' Chris became known at university as Christian Chris and whenever he went for a night out, he would end up in conversations with people about Jesus.

Pausing again to collect his thoughts, Chris said, 'A shift happened . . . I remained enthusiastic about getting people to come to faith but I realized events the CU were hosting were having nothing more than a negligible impact. I became very jaded.'

On top of that, Chris had his first encounters with church politics, consisting of a huge clash between two different groups supporting CUs. He could see the benefits of both and attempted to work with each one but political problems higher up meant that was not possible. Many people were upset by this.

I could hear the hurt in his voice. Chris took a moment to look up again at the grey clouds continuing to amass; it felt almost as if they were pressing down on us.

'I started to get disillusioned with CU, so basically I stopped going. I was actually quite bitter about it and decided I just wouldn't bother. I didn't question my faith and I was still going to church. Two in fact – one in the morning, one in the evening. But I felt like what was going on in regular churches just wasn't enough.'

During his role on the CU Exec, Chris had got involved in town prayer initiatives. He had felt God was asking him to pray for the town specifically. He had visited a 24–7 Boiler Room in Reading. 'There I saw free-flowing community, people coming and going, there was hospitality, creativity, prayer, working with local youth. It was very dynamic and I remember thinking this was way more like church I'd read about in the Bible than anything else I'd seen.'

Chris wanted to set up a similar prayer room in Bournemouth. He met people with a similar heart and in his last year at university, he helped launch a monthly prayer event. He shared the vision of a prayer room with church leaders but whereas they wanted to develop a culture of prayer, Chris remained focused on setting up a prayer space.

Church leadership seemed to move so slowly and it frustrated him. He took another mouthful of pasta and said, 'I didn't really know what it was to be led, to be under someone . . .' Eventually, Chris and his friends were commissioned to set up a prayer space but it failed to live up to his expectations. Every Friday night they would open the space for prayer. Chris would be there every week feeling something was not quite right but not knowing what.

Chris invested so much of his time, energy and prayer life into the prayer room but eventually left the project. 'It was a real sense of loss,' he explained, hesitating again to reflect on his memories.

'So what happened next? I mean, I guess you were pretty disillusioned after the prayer room project . . . ?' I said.

With a deep breath, Chris continued. He was upset with what had happened but at the same time he had joined a prophetic school and he was enthusiastic about

it. He started to develop a prophetic gift and to get some
quite accurate words of knowledge. God was using him
and he saw signs of healing that re-fuelled a desire for
evangelism. He remembered coming back from the
course and telling his non-Christian friends things like,
'This person was deaf and now they're not. What about
that then?' This was a good time for Chris.

'I was still attending two churches but the pastor at
one of them said I should only be involved in one, so I
went to his. He wanted to meet up and disciple me, but
it was odd. I didn't know what to talk about. So I was
going to his church and involved in this town-wide
stuff.'

Chris had developed a good network of church rela-
tionships across the town, independent from his church.
His church life was lived more through the week than
Sunday morning. The only reason he kept going on a
Sunday was so that when asked, 'Which church are you
at?' he had an answer.

He admitted to himself it was a rubbish reason for
going to church and so he stopped going. For a time it
was great. He desired to see church not just as a congregational Sunday morning thing but as something woven
into the fabric of life.

Chris found others who were thinking similarly and
started spending time with this group who'd also opted
out of congregational church. He quickly discovered
how badly they had been hurt by the church and a con-
sequent depth of bitterness and hurt.

Chris was quiet for a moment. 'I began to feel I could
not pray in the way I wanted to around them. There was
a lot of disdain towards me, a lot of cynicism, a feeling I
was too churchy. I opted out of congregational church and
ended up with an even more dysfunctional community.
But I also felt the people I had previously been hanging

out with were so stuck in their Sunday-morning box. It was just a very strange time, and in retrospect, I should have hung out with people that actually liked me.'

After university, Chris moved to London. He too had become cynical. He'd got sick of the cross-town politics, the hypocrisy, the spirit of empire rather than kingdom and it all seemed fake. He questioned the prophetic happenings he had seen, wondering how much it was him doing it and how much was actually the Holy Spirit. He began to reason parts of his faith away.

Living in a new city, he felt completely uninspired to go to church. He carried on praying but not in the way he had done. He still hoped that God would respond in some way. Generally, he felt forgotten. When he prayed, nothing was happening.

Immersed

Chris's faith journey was punctuated by community.

He came to faith through the community of his local youth group.

He discovered a sense of calling and purpose through the CU community.

Chris also struggled with his faith in community as he witnessed church politics, broken dreams and cynicism.

His story seems to be a longing for community, authentic community. And this longing is not just true of him but is something each of us has – the world is changing but the innate need for fellowship remains.

In our technologically rich age, communication has never been easier. We can text. We can Skype. We can call. We can email. We can snail mail. We can instant message. We can even talk face to face. And yet, perhaps, communication has never been so hard.

In our cities, meeting new people has never been easier. We can get acquainted with new people at work, in the bar, at the gym, speed dating, in an online forum, by knocking on our neighbour's door, by helping out at a local project. And yet many of us feel more alone than ever.

In the West, we are so wealthy with our plasma TVs, our full bellies, our throwaway clothes and our fancy new mobiles. And yet, as Mother Teresa said, 'Loneliness and the feeling of being unwanted is the most terrible poverty.'

Although so much has changed, the deep desire for community remains.

Chris's story came to a point where he felt 'forgotten' through a lack of community.

In *Urban Tribes*, Watters explores how young adults across the US have moved away from their parents and into cities. As they have moved into these urban areas, they have naturally rebuilt community structures.

He explains, 'My group of friends came together to tackle group projects such as painting a living room, critiquing someone's rough cut of a documentary, or caring for someone who had fallen ill. We moved each other's furniture, talked each other through break-ups, and attended each other's parent's funerals. Those who had money loaned it to those who didn't. Everything we owned, from books to tools to furniture to cars, was shared, or loaned or given away on an ongoing basis.'[25]

This sounds like authentic community and as I read his book, I couldn't help but be reminded of the passage in Acts:

> They devoted themselves to the apostles' teaching and to the fellowship, to the breaking of bread and to prayer. Everyone was filled with awe, and many wonders and miraculous

signs were done by the apostles. All the believers were together and had everything in common. Selling their possessions and goods, they gave to anyone as he had need. Every day they continued to meet together in the temple courts. They broke bread in their homes and ate together with glad and sincere hearts, praising God and enjoying the favour of all the people. And the Lord added to their number daily those who were being saved. (Acts 2:42–47)

Community is not just for the early church; God has given each of us this natural desire to belong. I love the way the writer of Genesis records the story of creation. In Genesis 1, describing the creative process, the writer continually uses the words 'good'. He, in fact, uses it seven times . . . good, good, good, good, good, good, good. He seems to be making a point about the beauty of creation. However, then there is a real jarring in Genesis 2 when he writes, 'It is *not* good for the man to be alone' (2:18). Not good.

God created us in his image. He created us as relational people. And when the church fails to build authentic community, we fail to provide for one of humanity's most basic needs.

This idea of community reoccurs throughout the God narrative. Community is a central part of the Jewish tradition. Jesus builds community with his disciples and as he commissions them, he commands them to 'baptize them in the name of the Father, of the Son and of the Holy Spirit'.

It is interesting that the word 'baptize' is the Greek word *baptizo*, meaning 'immerse'. Water baptism is crucial but what if Jesus was trying to refer to something else here too? What if he was challenging us to immerse people into Father, Son and Spirit community – Trinitarian community (and by that I mean loving community)?

Perhaps so much of our fruitful evangelism does not have long-lasting fruit because we fail to immerse people in this authentic community Chris longed for – this real, messy and costly community. Chris glimpsed something of authentic community in the 24–7 Boiler Room and was excited by this vision of what Christian family could look like.

Authentic community?

If we fail to build authentic Christian communities, then we will lose many more passionate Christians like Chris. Therefore, the pressing question is what constitutes authentic community.

For six months, I stopped attending church so I can understand many of Chris's gripes. I was still in full-time Christian work but I was tired of going to church. I wasn't losing my faith but I wanted something more.

As Chris was disillusioned when the CU evangelistic strategies failed, I too was disillusioned with church evangelistic strategies. I would earnestly pray and invite my friends along to church. After a considerable amount of nagging, they would turn up on a Sunday. I would think this would be it, that once inside the church, they would fall to their knees in repentance. Instead, they had a 'nice time' but wouldn't be over-keen to come again.

I could comprehend how Chris wanted his Christianity to break out of a Sunday-morning cage and be released into his whole life. The meeting was the focus, rather than the other six days of the week. Like Chris, I was yearning for authentic community and there are many more like us, people who don't want to go to church but who wanted to be the church. These people opt out of organized faith communities to adopt a much more fluid style of church.

Chris did just that. In his search for authentic community, he ditched meetings and spent time with others who had similar frustrations. Yet the reality of fluid church (the idea church should have almost no structure) is very different to the idealized utopia it can seem to be from a hard church pew. Chris discovered a depth of cynicism there; church deserters bitter from their experiences.

Very few people can maintain their relationship with God without any structure. Fluid church requires discipline and a depth of accountability. It is too easy to float off into the ether or to become bitter. We can all critique what is wrong with old models but it is much harder to harness this energy to build creative and positive expressions of Christian community.

After taking my six months out from church, I chose to plant a new congregation. It stemmed from this desire for authentic community. When I use the term authentic community I am talking about church built on relationships rather than on meetings; I am talking about church that cares for the poor and the lost more than church politics; I am talking about church that is honest, real and gritty; a community that shares life.[26]

As Shane Claiborne writes, 'if you ask the average person how Christians live, they are struck silent. We have not shown the world another way of doing life.'

Perhaps much of what I am writing is about re-discovering a more monastic community. The term monastic here means a community enriched by ancient rhythms of prayer as individuals choose to undergo life together, living outside the cultural norms of wider society.

Unlike historic monastic movements, this community is not hidden from the world but finds itself based directly in its mission. Chris's passion for community was not merely for community's sake but so as to engage with the world. Authentic Christian communities, therefore, have to impact humanity around them.

Chris had a tremendously active faith and as I considered his account I thought perhaps he had had his dreams dashed too many times: his dreams as an evangelist to see people come to faith through the CU; his dreams for the prayer room to impact the town; his dreams as a prophet to bring God's word to the broken.

Missional dreams are near impossible without community, and community without missional dreams is not authentically Christian. So if we want to help the activists like Chris find a home, we need to birth some novel expressions of community.

Jesus leadership

Chris's story is also about relationships with leaders. One of the key pitfalls in forming authentic community is the issue of leadership. In the modern mindset the leader directed others – yet in our post-modern world, leadership is much more about an individual who visualizes an alternative reality and rallies his friends to share in making that vision become reality.

We are all in some way leaders as we all have the ability to influence and impact others. We may readily fall into the trap of leading out of our titles – as pastor, home group leader or youth worker – but we must strive to lead out of who we are and who we represent. Our leadership must be rooted in a desire to watch others grow and develop.

The phrases Chris used in describing the leaders he knew are telling; like 'slow to act' and 'political'. A key moment for him appears to have been when he was forced to choose a church; he was not allowed to be a part of two churches.

During the interview he recollected a specific awkward attempt at discipling that took place over breakfast with his pastor. 'Leaders had regularly tried to take me under their wing,' he said, 'but I felt that I had to join them in their activity rather than them joining me in my context. I didn't want to be told what to do by someone who had never bothered to get to know who I am. Maybe I am still a bit bitter.'

The subtext of this seems to be he had come across lots of leaders who didn't inspire respect.

Chris describes one church leader who had been different. He refers to him as a mentor and he is still in touch with him today. 'There was something that attracted me to this guy – that made me want to let him in – something other leaders didn't have. He was transparent and open with me about his own struggles. I felt able to be entirely real with him and for it to be OK, because I felt like he wasn't interested in me because I was "a future leader" or "a project".'

This leader earned his leadership role rather than taking it for granted from his position. Jesus led in this way – not by boasting he was the Son of God but through his character. He led by the way he was real, by the way he loved, by the cause that framed his life, by the way he wanted his disciples to excel, and by the way he birthed authentic community.

The backslider . . .

The clouds looked as if they were ready to burst.

'And would you call it backsliding?' I asked.

'No, I think it was part of my growth,' Chris said.

His response was fascinating. I think I would have characterized him as a backslider – he was not going to church, he wasn't sharing his faith, he wasn't reading the Bible – he was simply hoping God would one day respond to his lonely prayers. Do we sometimes, in our desire to pigeonhole people, make unhelpful presumptions?

'I'm not sure I ever lost my faith, but I certainly skirted round the edges of it,' Chris continued. 'I do reckon it was part of my growth. It was a shame it happened. The turning point came when I met my girlfriend. I remember praying before I met her, "Lord, I pray I meet someone who loves Jesus more than I do." She does and she really encourages me a lot.'

Finishing off his last mouthful of pasta, he paused momentarily. 'I wouldn't have called it backsliding; I'd call it leading myself down a dead end. It was still very much the exploration of my faith and I think I would've got out of that place eventually. I still believed and I still had a faith of sorts but I didn't know what to do with it; I'd lost my passion and understanding of it.'

'My girlfriend wanted to go to church and I hated the idea. We had loads of arguments about church and leadership, but she helped me to see I needed to forgive some leaders and that really helped. Eventually I attended church with her and I felt the Holy Spirit sort some stuff out in me. I'd reached the point where I knew I needed to engage in some kind of Christian community for my own sanity and so I joined a new expression of church but I still found it hard to commit – I kept finding social things that were more interesting!'

The first droplets of rain began to spill from the clouds above. 'But I did commit and because this new expression of church provides space to ask questions and the fact you can be a bit rough and ready about your faith, has meant I am getting back on track.'

I smiled as the droplets became a downpour and we ran for cover.

Practical tips

- Encourage people who have lost their faith to remain part of the social aspect of your church community.
- There may be issues of hurt or broken dreams that need to be talked through. It is essential space is made for forgiveness.
- It may be more appropriate for people who are journeying back into relationship with God to come to small groups rather than church services so they can ask questions and be more honest than a church setting might allow.

7

Stepping Stones

A quiet summer evening in a small village pub. Alan sat opposite me on the wooden picnic bench wearing a black shirt that hugged his build. He had thick side burns that wrapped around his face and a gentle smile. His short mousy brown hair had been gelled upward at the front. His fading tan was from a recent trek in the mountains of Nepal.

Alan had been brought up in a Christian family, attending the village church with his two older brothers. He had found Sunday school boring but had enjoyed seeing his friends. Growing up, nearly every kid in his village went to church.

The family services were tiresome and Christianity didn't connect with him. 'At that age, you're not really taking stuff seriously,' he explained. Although one of his brothers stopped going when he was eight, Alan kept at it in order to see friends.

As Alan moved from his childhood to his teens, the church underwent a transformation from a quiet and settled traditional church to being more active and focused on youth work.

Alan explained that at the same point his parents had divorced, though they both remained committed

Christians. 'I guess a lot of people go through it. To me it seemed like a big deal, and it did coincide with a lot of change at church and the church did help me out a lot. I felt pretty loved and comforted by the church family – so I considered my youth leaders and mentors to be important to me at the time.'

He began spending more time at church, throwing himself into youth clubs, Bible studies, Sunday school, cell groups and events. He was still going predominantly for the social side of things but he did call himself a Christian. During worship he felt uplifted and he chose to get confirmed. 'Now I'm not sure that was God, otherwise why am I not still a Christian?'

He took a gulp from his cold beer. 'So how would you define being a Christian, when you were in your early teens?'

Alan smiled. 'I guess I kind of knew the technical words. I was being a disciple and I was witnessing. I'd been to the right talks and I thought I was a pretty good role model for other Christians. The way I lived my life and behaved towards my friends at school was to be an example of the way Jesus wanted me to live.'

After his confirmation, he continued to be involved in church life, becoming a youth leader. By his late teens he was running the Sunday school. He felt supported and guided and was learning new skills.

'So in your personal time were you reading the Bible and praying?' We ignored the tiny pub dog yapping around our ankles.

'Yeah, I was always aware I hadn't had the same experiences of God other people have had; such as gifts like tongues or prophesy, and I was very conscious of this and all the teaching was that if you spent time with God, soaking, then these things would come. So I spent a lot of time doing my own stuff to get to where I thought I should be.'

Alan thought by going to youth groups and attending prayer events, he would encounter God more tangibly. But whilst others were experiencing God and the charismatic gifts, he felt nothing. He had been told that these experiences could not be forced and although he didn't worry too much about it, there was always a desire for them. 'The pressure was always internal, from myself. No-one was fussed.'

At eighteen, with the pressure of exams, Alan palmed off his leadership roles and spent his Sundays studying. He stopped his personal prayer times too.

Concurrently, he decided to start sleeping with his Christian girlfriend. He made up his mind that he didn't see the issue of sex before marriage from a conventional Christian viewpoint. He thought of it as something like eating kosher, a relic of an Old Testament lifestyle choice.

The exams finished and summer consisted of lots of holidays. And then Alan left to go to university. Church activities had been put on the back burner. He went to university because he wasn't sure what else to do. He spent his time having fun, going out with friends and regularly seeing his girlfriend at a different university at weekends. He felt fulfilled. He tried the Christian Union but never felt part of it. He didn't try looking for a local church.

'Did anyone ever talk to you about the move and how to deal with your faith?'

'No, it was just assumed that anyone who took their faith seriously would find a way to move their faith forward wherever they were.'

Two months into the course and Alan suddenly became worried by the fact he hadn't been going to lectures or writing essays. The fun was over and he started to panic. By Easter he had officially dropped out of university. At the back of his mind he thought when he returned home he'd get back into the God stuff.

Back at home, Alan got a job at an airport, which he loved and although he had intended to go back to church, he had lost the habit of attending. He was still regularly visiting his girlfriend at weekends and so made his excuses.

The smell of cigarette smoke drifted over from a nearby table. I asked if his parents had talked to him about the state of his beliefs.

Alan took another gulp of beer, 'Well, I guess they thought I was taking a break seeing as I'd been so involved with stuff before uni. I was still hanging out with Christian mates and things like that. They probably thought it was a natural time for a break and a bit of a backseat, but it didn't matter to me at all.'

'A couple of years later I started to really review my faith and what I thought of it. I kind of consciously let the church thing slip by and as I wasn't so busy with it all, it gave me space to think things through and look at what I really believed and how important going to church was to me.'

Another swig of beer. 'I figured I was a Christian, but that it didn't really matter whether I was at church or not. Just because you're in a building or talking to the right people or going through the motions, does that make you a Christian? So I was revising my opinion and decided that a Christian was someone who calls Jesus saviour, and on some basic level I still believed that, so I convinced myself I was a Christian and church was a periphery, so long as I was behaving in the right way.'

Alan would have debates at work and over a couple of beers in the pub. He would argue for the existence of God and Jesus but against organized Christianity. 'I guess I was a sort of teenage punk, all church was doing was spouting misleading ideas and false hopes and ridiculous expectations. I didn't need that anymore.'

At this time Alan's eldest brother started to get sick. Alan's laid-back demeanour changed as he talked about his brother. He was a Christian and loved being active, especially doing sports. He was diagnosed with kidney failure at the age of twenty-six. After the diagnosis was confirmed, Alan started to review the idea of evil and why bad things happen to good people. He couldn't understand why this was happening to his brother who was such a strong Christian.

Alan and his brother had been close. He had been a Christian role model and when he got ill, Alan realized his issue was not just with church but with the very concept of God.

When his brother first became ill, they set up prayer chains. To support his mother, he even began praying with her weekly. Yet his brother's condition worsened. A failed transplant left him unable to walk properly. 'There was nerve damage and artery damage too. It was a bit of a medical saga. I was gutted.'

'He's always kept his faith throughout it all, and that's impressed me. He doesn't like talking about whether God exists though. I was having debates with my friends, and would ask Mum, but she'd kind of ignore my questions as she always says she's worried that if she questions it, she might lose something that works for her.'

Resting his hands on the table, he continued, his voice raw. 'My family who were Christians stayed with their faith, whereas I went the other way and decided that this instance was enough for me to prove I didn't need it anymore – especially if prayer is this strong weapon, and you've got six churches praying for you, you'd hope you would see some improvement – but here we are eight years down the line and he's still getting worse and worse and he is now getting fits. So if prayer is a powerful weapon, what are they comparing it to?'

Two years later Alan read the popular book Richard Dawkins's *The God Delusion* which consolidated his thinking. The argument he found particularly convincing was why would you ever start with the Bible as the Word of God if you were looking at whether God exists. Alan agreed with Dawkins that if you're examining it logically, you would never start with the foundation that the Bible is God's word.

Alan told his girlfriend about the book and she felt he had changed his opinion overnight. She encouraged him to read the counter-arguments so he could say he'd read both perspectives and therefore he read *The Dawkins Delusion* too.

'The issue with *The Dawkins Delusion* is the author was arguing from a Christian perspective that presumes certain premises. So things like: the Bible is the Word of God, the idea God is omnipotent and benevolent and stuff like that. If you disregard all your premises and start with a blank sheet, a logical approach, as far as I could see, it would never lead you towards the Bible. I don't really like Dawkins, but he does make that one really good point.'

'So is your key issue the Bible?' I said awkwardly.

'Yeah, it's a massive one. For example, I don't know any Christians who obey kosher rules but yet they stick by things listed alongside them in the Old Testament. I guess the question is "Where do you make the chop-off point?" That's where I started my journey, with the whole sex before marriage issue. Obviously different denominations have differing interpretations of the Bible and so I guess that pokes one hole in the authority of it.'

'Also, once you get out of the Christian mindset, you can really start looking at it in a more logical way. Why did I ever put any trust in this anyway? People try and share the historical background but I reckon, as soon as you leave the Christian perspective, it all starts to fall to pieces. It could all be a load of gibberish, written by several gibbers across several millennia. Like, if someone has found several different scrolls spread across the world and all of them said Julius Caesar was God, would it actually make him God? Just because several scrolls say so, it doesn't make a ridiculous claim true.'

Alan told me how his Christian friends gave him books on the existence of God. He liked the challenge and they started an impromptu book club to discuss the issues that arose.

'So do you come at Christianity with a scientific perspective now?' I asked.

'I guess so. Like I'm no genius, but I think I understand science well enough to have a good grasp of when something has the ring of truth about it and when something sounds like it's been researched properly. I came to the conclusion that Christianity, when looked at with an open mind, needs a massive leap of logic to be found true.'

Perfect adolescence

Alan appears to have been the perfect young person. He was going to youth group, attending church, helping with the Sunday school and was even reading his Bible at home. He was doing everything right. And it was not just in relation to church. Alan had done well at school and was off to university. The model young person.

It was interesting Alan didn't know why he went to university. He could not work out what else to do and so conformed to the expectations put upon him.

See, I wonder if Alan's faith was also about conformity. I wonder, with the expectations put upon him, whether he just did what he thought right, rather than asking his own questions. The local church was massively supportive but was Alan ever encouraged to share his views and to think for himself? Instead he had simply conformed. From his outer appearance in his teenage years, it seemed Alan was fully on track with God – yet behind the scenes, as he would admit, his faith was shallow.

There are many young people in our churches who simply conform. They join the worship band, they help out with the children's work and they give the impression of enjoying church activities. However, they do not really own their beliefs.

There came a point in my own faith journey when I realized for the first time my faith was my own faith and not merely that of my parents. I had to step out from my parents' shadow and discover my own relationship with God. This was a revelation for me. In order to do this, young people need opportunities to challenge and question, rather than conform.

As Alan shared his memories, it became clear he had always longed for a Holy Spirit experience. He wanted to prophesy or to speak in tongues and yet despite his faithfulness in attending church and reading his Bible, he never did. He did not talk through these frustrations.

I meet many young people, and many not-so-young people, who are desperate for a specific supernatural encounter to confirm their faith. We presume because someone has a specific gift, we should have that gift as well. We presume because someone cries when they are prayed for, we should cry too. We are an experience-hungry culture.

When we do not have the experiences of God others appear to have, frustration and doubts creep in. We forget we are all created to be different. One person's relationship with God will never be identical to another's. My worry is we are so experience driven we each want the same ones.

Throughout the Bible, people's times with God vary so much. Some people believe because of dramatic supernatural visions and others as the Gospel is simply preached.

I would expect Alan had in fact experienced God but that this was not validated. He is a scientific, pragmatic individual and his encounters with God may well not have come through tears and uncontrollable laughter. They may have instead come through a sense of God's peace; a moment of wonder at a sunset; sensing a depth of meaning in a biblical text; or the realization of the enormity of creation in a science lecture.

We are each unique and our relationship with God is unique.

Alan kept conforming until his faith and lifestyle conflicted. He decided to sleep with his girlfriend. The decision to do so may not seem a striking issue today but it was actually a decision to reform his understanding of the Christian way of life. With this decision, he was questioning the Scripture with which he had grown up.

From here, there are a series of stepping stones away from God. He stopped attending services and began to wonder whether church was necessary. He still claimed to follow Jesus but he felt the church was holding him back. He was drifting away from faith: then he was confronted with the harsh reality of his brother's sickness.

Prayer did not work. His brother got sicker. Therefore God did not work. The illness gave him permission to confess his disbelief. The reality of the hardship of life along with the diminishing expectations to conform meant Alan left Christianity.

Many young adults stop participating in church activities and leave their beliefs behind. It is imperative we help them navigate huge transitions effectively. Francis and Richter note in *Gone for Good?* that as people change location, job or peer group – or as they enter a new phase of life, like parenthood – they can often stop going to church. A life shift occurs, the support and expectation is removed and the individual's faith is tested.

Although transitions are tricky, possibly the most fundamental question is how do we allow young people brought up in the church to own their faith? How do we swap conformity for discipleship? How do we facilitate young people to have a unique relationship with God?

Losing my religion

As Alan relinquished his Christian heritage, he adopted a new worldview through reading Dawkins's *The God Delusion*. Alan likes science. The very term science comes from the Latin *scio* meaning 'to know' and Alan has a deep desire for knowledge and understanding. Dawkins's scathing attacks on the very notion of God's existence have solidified Alan's stance that Christianity is untrue.

In western culture, we pride ourselves on our knowledge of how things work. We reduce everything to the material level, to processes and formulas. Even our emotions are subsumed under chemical names. (For example, love has been broken down into three phrases: lust which is caused by hormones like testosterone and oestrogen; attraction which is caused by the release of chemical such as dopamine; and attachment which is related with oxytocin and vasopressin.) Does science have all the answers though?

My view of God has changed over the years. As a child, I think I imagined a stereotypical Father-Christmas-type figure, sat in the clouds. My perception was altered by discovering and reflecting on the different images the Bible gives us to understand God – images like Father, King, Creator, Judge and Lord.

As a child I believed I could understand God – but as my journey of faith progresses I realize time and time again that although all of these images are helpful, God remains mysterious. I know God but I also do not know him. I strive to know more of him but the more I know, the more I realize I do not know. I love that phrase, 'A God we could fully understand would not be big enough to meet all of our needs.'

Conceivably, part of Alan's problem with faith is that the church's view of God does not work for him. He wants to understand. His scientific studies had taught him to view things logically, to test out premises and to work with formulas.

He struggled when his formulaic reading of the Bible and time spent in prayer did not result in the encounters he desired.

He struggled when a loving, all-powerful God did not heal his brother. The six praying churches had not found the right prayer formula to produce miracles.

He struggled with Christian jargon that skirted around issues. He explained, 'There are these phrases like, "I don't know but God does" which is a pretty unconvincing argument when you're debating his existence. Others are, "Even if God explained it to me, I'm not sure I'd understand," and "Well, I believe it, and that's what's important to me." It always seems people don't know the answers and they don't seek out answers.'

I fear 'God is mysterious' might appear like another trite response.

So often Christianity is on the defensive but sometimes we need to be on the *offensive*. I am continually amazed by how much we can understand about our world through science. However, there are many questions that science fails to answer . . .

Science can't sufficiently explain to me why there is a longing to worship and a desire to connect with God.

Science can't sufficiently explain to me why I fall in love.

Science can't sufficiently explain to me my purpose and why I am here.

Science provides many answers about material things but a relationship with God answers many of the questions about hope, love, purpose, identity and spirituality. Yet a relationship with God does leave many questions unanswered because God is mysterious.

The answer 'God is mysterious' may appear patronizing to somebody wrestling with unanswered prayer and the 'Why do bad things happen to good people?' question. There are many questions we will have to our deathbeds though.

The challenge is, therefore, how do we teach the mystery of God in our churches? We teach the A, B and C of salvation which is clear and logical but we do away with the mystery of God. It is no wonder when we talk with such simplicity about the things of God that people believe God is simple to understand.

Many things remain a mystery to me about God today but I do have a relationship with him. He may not always answer my prayers the way I wish but I do believe he does answer them, that he supports me and sustains me when times are tough.

Alan spoke about Bible reading and saying prayers but not of a relationship with God. His brother, who has suffered immensely, still has a faith in God, despite the unanswered prayers. Is this the difference between relationship and religion?

It is good news God is found in relationship rather than formula: it means we have permission to be real with him. We can get angry and we can rejoice with him. We can cry and we can laugh with him. He is big enough, strong enough and loving enough for us to be real with him. Maybe we need, as the church, to rediscover something of his mystery?

The whole truth

Just because our faith is based on relationship doesn't mean we stop using our heads. God gave us an innate desire to think, to know and to understand.

We live in an age when experience dictates much of what we believe. People live by the rule, 'if it works, do it'; rather than, 'if it is an absolute truth, do it'. It does not demand much of us to base our faith on experiences of God and stop using our minds. Because of this we must not lose the ancient art of apologetics, defending our beliefs with argument and logic. As Christians, we must never stop learning, thinking and evaluating.

Alan enjoys debating concepts. Having read Dawkins, he wanted to know how Christians would respond to his new-found arguments. His arguments were about the validity of the Bible and his main frustration was Christians were unable to defend the Bible as the 'Word of God'.

The Apostle Paul was skilled at debate. He engaged people so well because he met people where they were at conceptually. When he debated with the Jews, he began with the Torah and when with the Greeks in Athens, he began with their cultural statue to the Unknown God (Acts 17).

Thus our discussion begins not in our presuppositions but where people like Alan actually are. We must start with their honest questions. Conversations with Alan could have begun with Dawkins's book rather than the Bible.

Alan said, 'At church it was always about how to use the Bible, rather than why we should build our lives on the Bible. We never discussed the arguments as to why the Bible is the Word of God; these intellectual arguments only ever came up in the pub.'

It saddens me intellectual discussions like this are sidelined to the pub. They should be part of what we do as Christian communities.

The Bible is the most amazing and complex book. About forty authors from all walks of life, from three continents, in three different languages contributed over a time span of 1,500 years. It is the foundation of Christianity and its authority is echoed though church history, creation and our experiences of God today. We must not sideline Scripture, we must instead defend it and wrestle with the challenges it delivers as we try and grasp God's redemptive story – a story that starts in Genesis and ends in Revelation.

It is wonderful that although Alan has left the church, the church has not deserted him. His Christian friends continue to engage with his questions. Together they have read *Letters from a Sceptic*, a book comprising of a series of letters between a father and son. The atheist father is encouraged by his son to write to him with any questions about Christianity and a dialogue commences.

This idea of exploring the difficult questions is an example of how we could re-engage with people who have left their faith. As Alan commented, 'I guess they think they are witnessing by loving me and continuing to hang out with me, even though we have different values and opinions. That is probably the best way and the best advert for Christianity – also the willingness to discuss their opinions with me and for them to listen to mine. I value their openness to challenges I throw at them too.'

How crucial intellectual discussion and the knowledge of the Bible's validity are! I know I never want to stop learning. There will be times when I will need to say I just do not know but I hope these challenges will spur me on to explore more of the mystery of God.

We cannot prove God and we can certainly never prove he loves someone. Yet when we use reason and debate, we can begin to remove some of the obstacles blocking someone from finding faith in God. Once these obstacles are removed, the person is left with the choice whether or not to take that step in accepting Jesus. This step is a step of faith. It is risky, and its worth cannot be proved, but with it, you enter into a relationship with God.

Two empty pint glasses

The dog was back at our feet yapping again. Alan looked down at it beneath the table.

I asked him how he would describe his relationship with Christianity today.

'Patchy at best,' he began. 'I understand why it's important to some people, like my brother. I think he would have crumbled without his faith by now. So it can give people a lot of strength, and it can also give people the opportunity for community and support and love. But with faith, I do take a bit of an exception, because the whole way the Christian church is set up to convert people is a little bit . . . it just seems a bit too much.'

'For me, if you have faith and beliefs, keep them, by all means, but don't try and make everyone think the same things as you. Especially as now I consider a lot to be untrue and it seems to me to be like spreading lies.'

I found the use of the word 'lies' hard to swallow but I could understand his views. He thought the Christian faith had no credible foundation. He was still searching for answers and Christianity hadn't worked for him.

With his friends journeying alongside him, demonstrating grace and delving into the awkward questions, I hope one day enough of the obstacles will be removed so he can make that final leap of faith and enter into a relationship with God.

Two pint glasses sat empty on the garden table: we were gone.

Practical tips

- Find the starting point of your friend's questions about God and start on an exploratory journey with him or her reading Christian and mainstream books together. If you think they are asking philosophical questions you can't comprehend, find someone else who might be willing to help them. Always share your opinions with grace!
- Do not assume you understand exactly why someone has lost their faith.
- If your friend still has some belief in God but is beginning to doubt, encourage them to be real with God about their frustration and confusion.

8

Slogan Needed

'I fell down and bawled my eyes out. I felt the Holy Spirit and I knew how awesome he was.'

This was Josh, aged thirteen, just wanting to know the truth about Jesus. Two years later he would be pronouncing the Shahadah Declaration, the Islamic statement of faith, in front of an entire London mosque. How is it possible to go from one to the other?

We were sitting in a pizza place, steaming pizzas in front of us. I had picked Josh up after work and he'd looked pleased to see me. He wore jogging bottoms and a big black jacket and sported a moustache. Josh was now sixteen and had a job for the summer in a warehouse packing medical supplies.

As we tucked into our food Josh started to tell me about growing up in a Christian family in south London. He has two brothers, both older than himself. 'When I was young, my mum and dad took me to church all the time; I was a good kid at church and made a lot of friends . . .'

Josh speaks with a real enthusiasm and uses his hands animatedly when he talks. His parents were both involved in church leadership and, although it was sometimes hard being by their side, he respected them as he knew they were helping people.

His black hat sat snugly around his head and he gave it a quick swivel as he continued. 'When I was growing up I would think, "What's the point of church?" I didn't really see it. I was also worried people at school would think I was a weirdo for going. It was quite boring, so I usually sat at the back, twiddling my thumbs. I thought the worship was rubbish . . . it was just boring.' Josh had attempted various schemes to get out of church, principally saying he was too tired and needed to lie in.

Josh spoke of his two older brothers, his respect for them evident. Both had been brought up attending church but they both rebelled. Sean, his oldest brother, went through some tough experiences, getting mixed up with drugs and crime. Josh remembers how it affected him. 'Well, it challenged me,' he said. 'I was scared. I was asking God to help him but I couldn't see the point. I was thinking, "Why is my brother doing this if God is amazing?" I think I knew God was working in my brother and that he was testing him but I still found it confusing.' (Since rebelling Sean has come back to faith and has spent time with various missionary agencies. His other brother Dan is not a worshipping Christian at this point.)

It was at thirteen that Josh gave his life to Christ. He had had enough of living in limbo and he just wanted to know the truth. 'I fell down and bawled my eyes out. I felt the Holy Spirit and I knew how awesome he was.'

Having made his choice to become a Christian, Josh concealed it at school. 'I kind of kept it a bit low. Most of my mates at school weren't Christians and they were getting into all the bad stuff. I was hanging around with the wrong people but I wanted to be like them. I knew that if I'd told them I was a Christian, they'd say, "You're an idiot man, don't be doing that."'

On one occasion a Christian friend came up to him and invited him to church in front of all his mates. He acted dismissively, publicly telling his friend he wasn't a Christian and then later finding him to say that he would go.

Josh explained the difficulties and complexities of modern-day school life in south London. He described the rougher kids and how everybody conforms to whatever they are doing. He told me stories of these 'rougher kids' sleeping with lots of girls, mugging people, using drugs and spending time with men in their twenties and thirties. He realized he was being drawn further and further away from what he knew God wanted him to do.

'At school I wanted to prove myself as a hard boy; but when I was at church, I was Josh. I wasn't a bad man, I was the real me.' As he grew in his relationship with God, he chose to avoid mixing with the rougher kids and instead befriended the two other Christians. As he put it, 'I'd man up and be strong about my faith.'

Josh went on to paint a vivid picture of multicultural Britain. 'There were different gangs. There was a Christian group which was tiny, probably about three of us, and there was also the Muslim group. People would stay in their groups at break and would be constantly looking around to see who was about to kick off. People from one religion didn't really hang around with people from a different religion.'

Things appeared to be on track for Josh but when he was fifteen some Muslim pupils started talking to him. He was confused as they were crossing the group boundaries. They asked him whether he would like to come to the mosque at some point.

At the time they asked, Josh was confused about God. God wasn't protecting him at school and he wasn't answering his prayers. At church he had begun sitting at the back again and he had stopped listening. In the end, he chose to go along one Friday after school. He was intrigued to discover whether Allah was more powerful than God.

Josh recounts the experience of entering the mosque. 'It was the day of big prayer, Juma, and there was this guy there, Ahmed – and he's the cleric. He sat me down and talked me through the procedures and their rules. Then he said to me, "Are you ready to take the Shahadah, the declaration to Allah?" So I was like, "Yeah" and that was the first time I went there. The Muslim faith is very straight on, so if you're gonna do it, you do it right there. There's no waiting, no praying about things first.'

Josh's story was fascinating. It seemed such a sudden shift – on the spur of the moment to choose to become a Muslim. As he finished his pizza, I asked if he was the only one his Muslim friends brought along.

'There was one other white boy and the rest were Asian Muslims; so there were only the two of us white boys there.' Josh replied. 'So the cleric took us to the front, and there were about fifty people there to say the Shadadah Declaration. I felt nervous; nervous about what I was going to say to Mum and Dad.'

'And did you want to say the Declaration?' I asked.

'I felt pressured but another part of me wanted to say it as I'd had enough of being a Christian. I didn't believe it was the right religion. If it was why didn't God answer my prayers?'

Josh went into more detail about stating the Shadadah Declaration. From the front of the Mosque he read it, some Arabic and some scripture from the Qur'an. Straight after everyone gave him a hug and they feasted.

He began going to mosque regularly after school, arriving home late. He would lie to his parents and say he had been at a friend's house. On one occasion he went to the town centre with friends from the mosque to set up a stall. He was taught to try and break up groups of

boys and have conversations when they were outnum-
bered (i.e. for the Muslims to outnumber the boys from
the streets). On the streets they had seen young people
become Muslims.

'It was very much like – pow – you're a Muslim – pow
– you've got these rules and you have got to do this and
this. I was like woah, yeah, I'll do it. So I was going to the
mosque and, basically, I was told to lie to people. I was
told I couldn't stay with my parents as they were
Christians, so I'd have to live somewhere else. I had to
get out of it by saying I was living at my brother's.'

Josh started to lead a dual life. He was secretly a
Muslim but his parents had no idea. As he read the
Qur'an, he realized he couldn't spend time with
Christians anymore. To commit to Islam, he needed to
push all his old friends away. He gradually stopped
communicating with Christians and although he would
still go to church with his parents, he would just sit at the
back or leave early.

Man up

The term 'man up' is becoming more and more common
amongst young people. The Urban Dictionary defines it
as being brave and strong, fulfilling your responsibilities as a man.[27] Josh's story is full of masculine language
and images. His journey from boyhood to manhood
is set amidst the growing gang culture of south London.
He wanted to be a 'hard boy' and it was time to 'man
up'.

My teenage years were spent wrestling with what it
meant to be a man. At weekends, depending on the mis-
chief you got up to, you could strut back into school on
a Monday morning crowned a man. If anything, that

pressure to prove yourself and your masculinity has become even greater.

Josh was wrestling with what it meant to be strong – to be brave – to have respect: to man up. His peers were modelling what they thought it was to be men but at church there was a lack of role models. Josh was also not interested in a 'boring' service with 'rubbish' worship music. Josh's family did include men living out their faith but his story still epitomizes a Christian male's struggle for identity.

Many men have stopped going to church. It's confusing in a way because most churches are led by men yet have a much higher percentage of women in their congregations. There is a range of arguments as to why this is the case. Some claim church services are too emotional; singing worship songs that are reminiscent of boy-band love ballads. Some argue services are too passive and that men want to 'do' rather than just spectate. Others claim that services fail to relate to men's lives; spiritualized teaching with no relevance to man's daily work, rest and play. (Please note that some of this section could arguably be applied to women.)

In a recent seminar run by Christian Vision for Men, we were given two sets of words. The first included the words: power, competency, achievement, success, accomplishment, targets and goals. The second list was: love, relationships, support, nurture, harmony, community and sharing. We were then asked which set best described the church. Almost everyone chose the second set. At this point the leader of the seminar informed us that according to *Men are from Mars, Women are from Venus* (the bestselling book on differences between the sexes) the first set of words were how men described themselves and the second set were how women did so.[28] There are clearly issues with how we do church.

However, perhaps the biggest issue is that we have feminized Jesus. We are taught we should become more like Jesus but for men, this translates as the need to become 'meek and mild'. This smacks in the face of contemporary masculinity.

Josh told me he had wanted to be a 'hard boy'. If he was like me in my adolescence, then this was a desire to be accepted as a man. As I mulled over my journey to manhood, I remembered how I had struggled to understand what it meant to be a man and a Christian. For me, being a man was about being strong and being a Christian was about being weak. I was taught the teaching of Jesus, to 'turn the other cheek' and I could picture young people like Josh doing just that, being beaten to a pulp and then feeling God had failed to protect them. I think I thought being a Christian man was about being a Christian doormat.

This difficulty in understanding what it is to be a Christian man is in part because we misinterpret meek as weak. The Greek word for meek is *praus* and it infers controlled strength. For example, whenever I drive up to traffic lights there is nothing stopping me from crossing a red light. The engine is running and I have the power to carry on but I stop if the light is on red. Meekness is just this. It is having the power and the strength but choosing to bring it under control.

Jesus was meek. As the Son of God, he had all the power in the world at his disposal and yet he chose not to use it, but instead to fulfil the mission to go to the cross.

Christian men are therefore called not to be weak, but to be meek. They are called to follow the Jesus who wept and welcomed children but also the Jesus who turned over tables and made a whip when he got angry; who spent much time mixing with other men; who fasted forty days; who bravely prayed 'Yet not my will, but yours be done' with sweat on his brow; who had the audacity to stand up to the leaders of his day demanding justice for the marginalized. Jesus embodies bravery, boldness and strength.

This is the kind of role model for which men are looking. We need to re-focus on the masculinity of Jesus.

When Jesus spoke about turning the other cheek, he was not calling us to be passive. At the time, social etiquette meant you would not hit someone with your left hand as that was used for 'unclean' things: you would use your right hand. The initial blow would have been a backhanded hit, not to cause pain but to dishonour. By turning the other cheek, the attacker could not hit you with his backhand again. Instead he would have to slap you with the front of his hand or punch you. Now only equals fought in this manner. Thus, you were making your attacker publicly acknowledge you as an equal, if they chose to hit you again. With this understanding of the cultural context, we discover Jesus was, in fact, being proactive.

This model of Jesus as a proactive man with controlled strength helps us embrace much of what it is to be a man. The problem remains that at school, standing up as a Christian is difficult. It's daunting going against the crowd whilst you are wrestling with all of the troubles of adolescence.

Josh had tried to live out his faith but then he was invited to the mosque. This wasn't just an invitation to the mosque; it was an invitation into a brotherhood.

It is hard to comprehend what it must have been like for Josh as he walked to the front of the mosque and went through the rituals of becoming a Muslim. I get the impression he was both fearful and excited. He knew there would be implications for the choice he was making and yet Islam seemed to have lots of answers. Islam recognized Josh as a man. Islam gave him a brotherhood to which to belong. Islam gave him structure. Islam meant that he no longer had to fear being bullied at school. Islam was masculine. Islam gave him a cause.

Rebels with or without a cause?

In 1992, hundreds and then thousands of cyclists began to gather monthly in San Francisco to cycle together through the streets. They caused chaos as streams of them whizzed down main roads, engulfing the urban environment. Since then Critical Masses, as they have become known, have taken place across the globe.[29] When they first began, nobody seemed to comprehend their purpose. Were they protests against polluting cars? Were they a celebration of cycling? Were they an assertion of cyclist's rights?

These word-of-mouth gatherings of cyclists got on national TV shows and on one report a few hundred participants were filmed blocking an inner city tunnel, shouting 'We need a slogan!'[30]

There is something powerful in that phrase 'We need a slogan!'

I grew up, like Josh, with Christian parents.

There are many good things about having Christian parents; the bedrock of faith they model is incredible. Yet every young person needs to discover their own identity and this involves rubbing up against the world. There is a natural tendency to want to rebel against the things that our parents have stood for. For me, my parents' Christianity was an easy target. I wanted a cause and their religion failed to give me one.

I recently spoke at a university Christian Union event and one hall of residence had Che Guevara's picture emblazoned on the wall. It fascinated me that more than forty years after his death Che remains one of the few leaders who have become iconic figures. (Others include Mother Theresa and Martin Luther King Jr.)

Chatting to the students, I discovered they saw Che as a hero worthy of gracing their wall. In 2000, he was voted one of the twentieth century's most influential leaders and his face is the most replicated image in history; he adorns not only students' walls but posters, key rings, T-shirts and art galleries; he is sung about, written about and his life story has recently been re-told in a two-part film. What was it that inspired these students to see him as such a hero?

Arguably, it was the fact Che had a cause – and a slogan.

He was committed to uniting people against imperialism and pursuing Marxist ideals. His cause was bigger than himself and he believed 'Wherever death may surprise us, let it be welcome, provided that this, our battle cry has reached even one receptive ear'.[31] The revolution cost him his life and his final words of defiance were 'Shoot, coward, you're only going to kill a man.' He was shot and buried anonymously with his hands cut off by the superpower of his day.

Che remains an icon because he lived and died for a purpose he believed in. A generation today seem to be lacking a cause and I wonder if part of Josh's abandonment of Christianity was the need for one. In becoming men, we don't want just to talk and reflect: we want to act.

It is said that until you have found something worth dying for, you have not found anything worth living for. Materialism is not a cause. Celebrity is not a cause. Attending church is not a cause. This generation, like generations before, needs a purpose. Their lives embody that phrase, 'We need a slogan!'

Josh was sat at the back of the church twiddling his thumbs. He had not been mobilized for something larger than his life. And Josh is like many other young people lining our pews on Sundays. We ask these young people to lay down their sin at the cross but we fail to ask them to pick up a cause.

When we spend our lives focused on frantically trying to rid ourselves of sin, sin becomes an even bigger obstacle. Yet when we discover a purpose that captures our hearts, issues of sin seem to subside.

Jesus came with a cause, a revolutionary cause. Like Che, he lived for it and was martyred by the superpower of his day, with words of defiance on his lips, 'Father, forgive them, for they do not know what they are doing' (Lk. 23:34). Whereas Che's physically violent revolution was focused on Marxist ideals, Jesus' spiritually violent revolution started with the human heart and was focused on a new kingdom.[32]

When Jesus preached the kingdom of God was at hand, people got excited: a new reality was being birthed.

Painting a kingdom vision

Two thousand years on, the kingdom is still at hand. Jesus' manifesto, 'to preach good news to the poor . . . to proclaim freedom for the prisoners and recovery of sight for the blind, to release the oppressed, to proclaim the year of the Lord's favour' (Lk. 4:18–19), is now our manifesto. God's redemptive plans are in full swing and we, as ordinary people, are called to this kingdom cause.

When I was a child the Christian faith seemed to be about having a meal ticket to heaven. Like a golden ticket to Willy Wonka's factory, I believed my faith in

Jesus was about dying and going to heaven. Now, don't get me wrong, I am still looking forward to an eternity with Christ, where there will be no tears and suffering, but the kingdom cause is not just about me and my golden ticket. The kingdom cause is about grasping God's perspective of how things should be and partnering in his plans to put things back this way: your kingdom come, your will be done.

The kingdom cause is all about sharing our faith and seeing others enter a relationship with God. It's about living lives that demand explanation, loving others and boldly sharing the message of Jesus.

The kingdom is about justice: caring for the poor and sharing what we have. It is about challenging systems of injustice and breaking the chains of poverty.

The kingdom is about healing: praying for the sick, building one another up and forming community where we all are valued.

The kingdom is about the environment: living simply, re-discovering the connections to the planet God has given us and preserving all that was created good.

Imagine more of the kingdom breaking out! This is the cause worth living for. This is the cause worth dying for, to get excited about.

However, so often we fail to commission people to play their part. We fail to paint a picture of what can be. We become half empty rather than half full. We narrow our faith to committee meetings and maintenance mentality. And when we fail to live for the kingdom cause, the church fails to lead and others hijack our cause.

A recent article on the Guardian website claimed the British demographic leaving the church seems to be the same group swelling the ranks of the environmental movement. If the church neglects to paint a vision of the kingdom, our very vision will get hijacked by other groups. This makes me desperately sad.

When Josh came to faith, how could we have empowered him to find his place in our commission?

We can easily live in fear of other religions but if we paint kingdom vision and invite others to join us, then they will. Everybody is looking for a slogan – let's give them the kingdom slogan.

Manhood

Our plates were littered with cold pizza crusts. Our glasses were empty.

Josh was now telling me he had been made to keep going to church.

Three months on, he was still living a dual life: Muslim at school, Christian façade at home. 'I felt something on me every time I went to church, but I ignored it and pushed it out. I couldn't be bothered.'

'Then this one day, me and my brothers went to a café for a fry up. I love fry ups,' he grinned. 'Still no one knew I was a Muslim and my brother just said, "Josh, are you a Muslim?" I had a big mouthful of food and I wanted to spit it out and shout "What?" but I didn't, I just sat back and said, "No, no, no, no . . . of course not." And then I leant forward and said, "Yeah, I am."'

As Josh confessed his Christian brother nearly broke down and cried. At home he showed his brother all of his books on Islam, his suit and his kufe (hat), concealed under his bed.

'So how did your brother know?' I queried.

Josh smiled. 'I asked him and he said "Someone told me." And I was like, no, no, no. And then he said, "If you want to know the truth, God told me." I was like, "No, he didn't; your God tells you nothing. I know that 'cause he told me nothing when I was a Christian."' Josh refused to believe that God had spoken prophetically to his brother.

In the coming weeks his parents found out too. They were bitterly upset. Josh explained how his mother was tempted to throw him out but she told him she loved him too much to do so. She chose to allow him to make his own choices. Josh's father took him to talk through Islam and Christianity with a Christian expert.

'This guy answered most of the questions I had and helped me understand all this stuff but I felt trapped.' He agreed to go to a Christian summer festival and whilst he was there he received a call from the cleric who asked him, 'Where are you? It's Friday prayers.' Josh lied, explaining he was on holiday in Spain. Then, a couple of nights later, Josh saw the Holy Spirit at work.

'People were falling over, people were getting healed, giving their lives to Christ. So by this point I'd had enough and wanted to go home. I went outside for a bit of a breather. This was the first time I'd seen full on what God was about. People talked to me, but I didn't want to know, I stood firm for my religion. They tried to get me to come in and eventually I did. I said, "I don't want you to pray for me or nothing, but I'll come in and just sit down." I went through the entrance and lay down and sobbed. Someone came over and prayed for me and I was shaking – in my head I didn't believe God would forgive me, but I knew he had forgiven me as all my burdens were lifted. I was Josh again.'

Having committed to follow Jesus again, Josh had to face going back to school. 'I was really worried about telling my Muslim brothers because I thought they might beat me up. I went to school and told one of the guys and he just looked at me for a minute but after that he went, "That's alright, but why are you telling me, I don't want to know." After school, as I walked out of the gate, they were shouting names at me like Virgin Boy as that's what they called people that turned to Christianity.'

Josh's return to faith was due to a number of factors. Several people played a part: his brother with his word of knowledge; the conversation with his father's friend about Islam and Christianity; his parents' patience and persistence – and then the reality of God's Spirit.

As we came to the end of the interview Josh began to tell me about his plans for a skateboard mission. He sparked with excitement as he shared his dreams and his vision to see others meet Jesus. Not only had he re-found his identity as Josh through his relationship with God: he had also found a cause.

The journey had been arduous. Yet now Josh had his first summer job and a part to play in the Cause: he had become not just a man but a man with a role to play.

Practical tips

- It may be appropriate to find a kingdom cause (such as a conservation project or a fundraising appeal) you can encourage people who have lost their faith to take part in.
- With teenage boys, it may be useful to create some kind of rites-of-passage experience that involves looking at the masculinity of Jesus whilst taking an outward-bound adventure.
- If there is a specific stumbling block, such as another faith, then try and find a specialist who can talk through the Christian perspective.

9

The Impostor

It was a light spring evening. I could see the shadows moving through the glass panels of the front door before Tom opened it wide.

'Hey mate, good to meet ya!' came the unfamiliar Aussie accent. He grabbed my hand and his firm handshake was somehow very welcoming.

The semi-detached house seemed awash with noise. I was directed into the sitting room to meet Tom's wife, Naomi. She smiled radiantly at me as their two-year-old daughter laughed and jumped around.

'So what's this book about?' she asked.

Having given a brief synopsis, I followed Tom into the adjoining dining room. We sat at the table, with two cups of tea dividing us. Tom warmed his hands on his mug as I took out my notepad.

Tom has a broad build which was accentuated by his grey T-shirt. He is in his early thirties and has fine dark hair. He awaited my first question intently.

Tom grew up in Sydney, Australia with two brothers. His family were Salvation Army, or 'Salvos', as he affectionately calls them. His father was a bandsman who would wear full uniform and often share his testimony at open-air events.

With contemplative pauses, Tom related that when he was twelve his parents split up. After the break up, Tom moved with his mum and his brothers to Brisbane to be closer to relatives. His family were quite reserved and faith was seen as a private matter.

It was during the separation that his father gradually left the Salvation Army. 'I don't know why but he just packed it all in. He seemed to have a faith but then he just walked away from the whole Christianity thing.' Tom was puzzled by how quickly his father's Christian commitment diminished.

School was a mixed bag. On the one hand, Tom discovered he was academically very able. He was moved to the top class as he achieved excellent marks. However he struggled with the social aspect of school. Tom spent a lot of time on his own. The change of class meant he had left his friends and with the concurrent turmoil at home, he found it hard to make new friends.

Tom then recalled how he was bullied. 'Being a Christian didn't help me win any popularity contests,' he laughed.

And so, Tom became devoted to learning. In this area he could excel. He often found himself distracted at school but he quickly learned he could teach himself at home. He became an extremely competent self-motivated learner. His exam results were testimony to this.

'It's these childhood experiences that formed me. I became a fiercely strong individual, quite hard. I don't put up with crap. I speak how I feel.' Tom stated.

Throughout his teenage years, he kept going to church. And, as his intellect developed, his understanding of God became intellectually focused.

'There was no epiphany moment . . .' Everyone else at church had a date written in the front of their Bible to commemorate the date they became a Christian. But for

Tom there was no such moment. The front of his Bible had no date scrawled in it. And this concerned him. He felt he had drifted into a faith, a faith that was very impersonal.

This lack of a conversion moment meant Tom raised his hand and came forward to accept Christ at every available opportunity; at rallies, youth meetings and summer camps. But nothing seemed to change. There was still no moment of revelation. Doubts began to fester.

Tom went on to university to study IT and Engineering. As our conversation meandered through a series of tangents, his academic ability was evident. He speaks in a precise manner with a depth of concentration.

At university he continued to excel. Throughout this time, Tom kept going to church but he hadn't made any connection with the Christian student groups on campus. None of his friends shared his faith and Tom had no one to talk to about intellect and faith. Whereas his younger brother's faith flourished when he connected with other Christian students, Tom remained plagued with doubts and questions. He was alone and had no one with whom to share his struggles.

In his early twenties Tom had one of his first moments of clarity regarding his beliefs. His Bible study leader, an elderly Scottish woman, had agreed to sit down with Tom to talk through his doubts, particularly on whether or not he was actually a Christian. Having heard some of them through, she turned to him saying 'Tom, come on! Imagine this Bible is Jesus. I am trying to give it to you . . . will you accept it?'

Tom grabbed the Bible without hesitation. Immediately he felt a deep sense of joy and peace. This simple exercise helped to alleviate his concerns. In that moment he suddenly had a greater certainty that he was a Christian.

However, despite that defining moment, he was still plagued with doubt over whether or not God actually existed.

Tom doesn't do things by halves. If Christianity was real, he wanted to live it out in every aspect of his life. Yet he felt he had to be 100 per cent certain before committing himself fully. He also wanted to be honest, and these questions about whether God existed were eating away at his fragile faith.

Although he continued to diligently attend church, secretly he began to feel like he was becoming an imposter. The doubts and questions continued to swirl around his thoughts and he would often ask, 'Are you actually there God?'

Even though Tom was sharing his private thoughts and doubts, people still saw him in light of his commitment to the Salvation Army. They saw him as a man who understood theology and as a man of true faith. It was almost as if other Christians couldn't acknowledge and engage with his doubts.

One summer, at the end of a Salvation Army camp, people were asked to write encouraging words for one person on slips of paper. These slips of paper were then given to the named individual. When Tom received his snippets of paper, time and time again, people had written phrases praising his faith. Phrases like, 'I am really encouraged by the strength of your faith.'

When Tom read these, he was confronted with his doubts in an almost tangible way. He couldn't understand why people would say such things about him. From his perspective, he was brimming with doubt. If others thought he had a strong faith, he surmised, then maybe no one actually had a strong faith. Maybe the entire Christian faith is a sham, he pondered . . . an inadvertent conspiracy of people propping each other up, deluding each other about life's biggest questions?

And then, a while later, when Tom returned to his small home church, he was asked to become the youth group leader. The church leadership had also seen him as a man of faith, even though he had told them his doubts.

He felt he was completely the wrong person. How could he lead others when he was not sure he actually knew the way? 'I didn't think I was putting on a front but this request was impossible. I still had all these questions. I could teach good theology and create community but my faith was full of doubt,' Tom reminisced.

The serious atmosphere was suddenly interrupted as his tiny daughter burst into the room and ran to him to give him a hug. Tom beamed. And then, as quickly as she had come, she ran out again.

Tom's face became focused once more as he talked of how he had looked at other faiths. 'But no matter what I researched, the character and the life of Jesus remained so much more compelling. I kept coming back to Christianity.'

He also spent time analysing what the world had to offer. His father had left his Christian faith in pursuit of wealth. He had become a successful businessman who believed Christianity was merely a good framework for young men to discover decent morals. Tom had seen some of his university friends chose a much more hedonistic approach to life, yet, as he looked at the lives of his father and friends, he knew that wealth and hedonism would not satisfy him fully.

Christianity made coherent sense. It made sense of the human condition and the human need. It made sense on paper – however, Tom was not fulfilled. He was dissatisfied with a faith that was still riddled with questions.

Tom continued to meet with wise and learned people, fellow intellectuals who would talk through issues of faith. Their answers were good. Logically things made sense. But his dissatisfaction remained.

Frustrated, he began to lead life on autopilot. He was doing his best to live out his faith even though he felt nothing. He was still involved in the church but he was disappointed that the gospel didn't feel truly real.

This dissatisfaction became mixed with a feeling of condemnation. One day, whilst Tom was practising with the worship band, a conversation arose about Calvinism (the concept that certain people are chosen from before the beginning of time to be 'saved' by God). The keyboardist cited biblical proof texts to back up this position and Tom took the opposing viewpoint. The conversation quickly became an argument.

This had been a pivotal moment in understanding how he comprehended God's view of him. Immediately Tom felt underlying concerns about his exclusion, rather than acceptance by God, were confirmed. 'I mean, I thought, why would God choose me? Perhaps this is why I feel nothing, because he is ignoring me.'

Tom wanted a perfect faith. As he meditated on the Parable of the Sower, Tom saw his belief as the seeds that were scorched by the sun or eaten by the birds. He compared his personal faith to the great Christian martyrs and felt his was just not real. Subconsciously, he believed that only with a perfect faith could he achieve and know God's love.

He felt that his doubts were robbing him of God's acceptance. Christianity made logical sense but there were only just enough moments of spiritual clarity to stop him leaving completely.

The undercurrent

I love watching the ocean. From the safety of the shore, you can often identify which way the water appears to be moving. Yet beneath the surface, undercurrents can form. These undercurrents typically run in the opposite direction to those on the surface. They can start unexpectedly and sometimes travel even faster than the surface currents.

Tom was committed to the church. He helped out in the worship band and served at summer camps. He read his Bible and he prayed. On the surface, Tom appeared to have it all together. But beneath the surface, an undercurrent of doubt and disappointment was eating away at his delicate faith.

Tom never fully lost his faith. It may appear strange to have his story amongst these chapters but Tom's story connects with many churchgoers today. On the surface, everything looks calm but beneath the surface, some of us are wrestling with similar undercurrents of doubt, uncertainty and dissatisfaction. And because everything looks okay, the undercurrent is never dealt with.

Doubt is a very real part of our faith because faith is relative certainty. Faith is *not* absolute certainty. The existence of God can never be fully proven and a real faith will have moments of doubt and questioning. However, faith is not relative uncertainty either. Faith is not just a matter of intellect, a matter of will or a matter of emotion. Faith is grounded in the evidence surrounding us.

John Wesley suggested a framework for understanding God using four building blocks. Firstly, and most importantly, we build our faith on understanding Scripture. It is in Scripture we discover how God has revealed himself through history. Secondly, we build faith in experiencing God, whether in the awesomeness of creation or through the complexity of our emotions. Thirdly, we use reason to logically work through our faith. Finally, we build faith as we look at church history. All four elements provide checks and counterbalances as we grapple with what it means to be people of faith.

Where there is faith, there will be moments of doubt. We need to rob the undercurrent of doubt of its power. We do this by giving each other permission to express doubt. Tom thought he was all alone. He also thought theat he needed a perfect faith, free from all doubt. Although he had spent time logically working through his questions with theologians, he had never been granted an opportunity to express his continuing doubts.

There have been times in my life when I have doubted. I have wondered whether my beliefs are just a result of my upbringing. Talking through my questions has been essential. However, when faith becomes solely focused on our inward questions, we are losing something of what faith is all about.

Faith is not merely an internal belief system. Faith, on whatever level, must move us to live differently. Faith requires action. Or as James explains it, 'faith without works is dead' (Jas 2:17).

Faith is risky and in my times of doubt, I have purposely sought to find new outlets to express whatever level of faith I still have. At these times, I have asked God to speak to me and I have actively listened, spending time in silence. When I sense the undercurrent of doubt, I have challenged myself to push beyond my comfort zone, to express God's love and to pray for others. These actions go against every natural urge but it is in these instances that my beliefs have been revitalized as I have seen something more of God.

Doing this helps to take the focus off me and put it squarely back on God.

Faith is like breathing. As we breathe in, faith is about receiving from God, knowing more of his love. We must also breathe out and exhaling represents expressing our faith in action. Some of us need to learn to inhale; some of us need to learn to exhale.

Three is the Perfect Number

Faith in God. Simple.

Tom's story made me reflect on how we often talk about faith in God. What we are actually talking about is not only a faith in God but a faith in the character of God. Faith in God is faith in his love and his holiness.

Since the earliest Christian creeds, we have understood God in terms of the Trinity; the Father, the Son and the Holy Spirit. Very often our church traditions focus on just one of these three aspects of God. From listening to Tom's story, he had a depth of understanding of Jesus. Jesus was preached in his local congregation week in, week out. During our conversation Tom explained how he had never really learned about Abba God or the Holy Spirit.

Our understanding of the character of God will deeply influence how we live out our faith. It is key to be aware of God in terms of the Trinity. What if some of our doubts arise from a slanted understanding of the character of God?

Without faith in the Father, we can easily forget the enormity, the power and the sovereignty of God. We can forget God is big enough to take care of us and big enough to deal with our issues.

Without faith in Jesus, we can easily forget the sacrifice, the humility and the example of God. We can forget God knows what it is to be human, to suffer and to be tested.

Without faith in the Holy Spirit, we can easily forget the presence, the holiness and the equipping of God. We can forget God is still at work in the world, transforming us and enabling us to join in his mission.

Backstage

Having witnessed his parents' divorce, Tom chose not to get married. He detached himself emotionally from the possibility. That was, of course, until he met Ang.

Naomi is the polar opposite to Tom. Tom is an introvert; Naomi is an extrovert. Tom thinks things through; Naomi lets her emotions lead her. Tom was brought up in the church; Naomi came to faith as a teenager through a friend.

They met at the local Salvation Army church, where they dated for four years before getting married. It was this relationship that was critical in helping Tom galvanize his faith. During his struggles, he had always sought counsel from fellow intellectuals. Naomi's faith wasn't primarily built upon logical deduction. Her faith was built upon a relationship with God. She gave him a different perspective.

When Tom would wallow in doubt, Naomi would sometimes give him a sound talking-to. She encouraged him to remember and commemorate what God had done in his life: the simple answers to prayer; the moments when God had felt close; and the times when there was clarity in his faith.

Tom explained, 'Often in the western mindset, we rationalize everything. And while there is evidence for God one day, we try and rationalize it away the next. But now I have begun to see God's work throughout my life.'

He said he could now see how God had been working in his life at university and in finding a job and in marrying Naomi. He had sensed God's direction when he was suddenly made redundant. Seemingly ordinary conversations had a divine sense behind them. It was these   conversations that had led him to Britain.

When they arrived in the UK, it was difficult to find a church. Then, one day, at the supermarket, Tom overheard a conversation between two shoppers about a local church. Having heard their conversation, he checked out the place they had mentioned. He felt immediately at home there. One of the first sermons there was on the verse promising that 'You will do greater things than these . . .' The preacher went on to speak with honesty about his dissatisfaction with not seeing these 'greater things'.

The church was on a journey that helped Tom discover the works of the Holy Spirit. He discerned he had made God in the image of his own father and gradually began to see God as his Daddy. The Holy Spirit became more real to him. He was healed of some of his childhood experiences. And he began to see God doing miracles. He witnessed a friend, struck down with ME for years, receive partial, and then full, healing. He had seen another friend suffering with irritable bowel syndrome healed and able to eat pizza and drink beer again. Yet another, known as Shaky Dave, had late onset Parkinson's. The doctors could do nothing more for him but then, through prayer, Shaky Dave was healed and re-named Rock Solid Dave.

Having related these amazing events, Tom systematically talked through what had happened in his discovery of a deeper sense of faith.

Firstly, being married to Naomi meant he had grown emotionally. He had experienced joy and had begun to understand his faith from a new perspective. Secondly, the birth of his daughter had given him a revelation of unconditional love. Tom had started to understand just how God saw him. Thirdly, he had stopped trying to have a perfect faith. He had recognized having faith meant having doubts at times. Lastly, he had ceased striving and had discovered, first and foremost, God wanted a relationship with him.

Feeling the interview had come to a natural end, I asked, 'So do you think God had been working behind the scenes throughout?'

'Yes, I guess. Don't get me wrong, there are still lots of questions. But now I am confident I will get the answers I need. The things I don't need, I will not fully grasp – but I have a peace in that. And I still want to feel more of God but I am comfortable with my faith in God right now. I am resting in him.'

Practical tips

- If your friend is struggling with belief, encourage him or her to talk through doubts with someone who has a similar personality type, as well as someone who approaches faith in a very different way.
- Help friends who are struggling with faith to explore an aspect of the Trinity they have not done before.
- It may help to logically work through Wesley's four building blocks for faith – Scripture, Experience, Reason and Church Tradition.

Epilogue

Finding Faith

Simple mathematics and war heroes

I regularly receive newsletters from a variety of Christian organisations, sharing exciting news of high numbers of people responding to Christ at different events and through various courses. It would appear from these letters the church is enjoying boom time – that revival is here.

And yet, at the same time, newspapers suggest the church is in terminal decline. 'Church attendance in Britain is declining so fast that the number of regular churchgoers will be fewer than those attending mosques within a generation . . .' read one report in *The Times*.[34]

This kind of article seems to be re-enforced by the sight of the boarded-up church buildings that are quickly redeveloped into fashionable apartments or smart new nightclubs. There often appears little hope as society drifts seamlessly away from our Christian heritage to adopt a more pluralistic worldview devoid of Truth.

So what is going on? Are we in revival or facing terminal decline?

It appears God is doing many great things but, as many people come to faith, others leave it.

Jim Collins, in his book *Good to Great* tells a remarkable story about Admiral Jim Stockdale, one of the highest-ranked American military officers captured in Vietnam during the conflict. He was tortured over twenty times in his eight years at the 'Hanoi Hilton' prisoner of war camp. His story is one of a military hero, supporting fellow captors whilst suffering intense brutality without knowing if he would ever be released. He remained loyal to the US and purposefully disfigured himself with a stool and a razor blade so he could not be televised as a well-treated prisoner. He became an American hero.

When Jim Collins met Stockdale, he asked him who didn't make it out of the camps. Stockdale simply replied, 'The optimists'. It was those that kept believing they would be out by Christmas, and then Easter and then Thanksgiving, who died in prison of broken hearts.

Collins coined the phrase the Stockdale Paradox as a fundamental key for turning companies from good to great. This paradox contains an important lesson for the church today. The Stockdale Paradox argues 'You must retain faith that you will prevail in the end and you must also confront the most brutal facts of your current reality.'

We need to remain a people of hope, a people expectant for what God will do but at the same time we must confront the painful facts of our reality.[35]

A heifer, a goat, a ram and some birds . . .

When I wandered away from Christianity, many people gave up on me. They stopped believing I would ever return. I am sure people thought the same about individuals such as Bethan or Kris.

It's easy to lose hope, to become disillusioned and to simply give up.

One of my favourite Old Testament stories is about Abram (Gen. 15). God gives him this incredible promise that he will have as many descendants as there are stars in the sky. God then commands him to gather a three-year-old heifer, a three-year-old goat, a three-year-old ram, a turtledove, and a young pigeon. It appears a random request today but Abram knows what is happening.

With no further instructions, he cuts the animals in two, leaving a bloody trail between the carcasses. He understands God is asking him to prepare for a covenant ritual. At that time, whenever you conquered an enemy, you would make them walk this bloody trail as a sign of their covenant and commitment to you.

As Abram kills these animals, I presume he was expecting God to make him walk through the carcasses, thus demonstrating his commitment to God. But then God does something quite incredible. He sends Abram into a deep sleep and a flaming torch appears. The flames symbolize God and slowly move between the carcasses. In this instance, God is not asking Abram to commit to him; he is actually showing his commitment to Abram.

God's commitment to us now is not based upon bloody animal carcasses but upon the life, death and resurrection of Jesus. Jesus' blood sacrifice reminds us he remains more committed to us than we ever can be to him. God is also more committed to the individuals in this book than we ever can be. God longs to draw them closer to him. If God is committed and does not give up, then neither should we . . .

Luke recounts a story Jesus told in his gospel. A woman who has ten pieces of silver loses one and so lights a lamp, sweeps the house, and seeks diligently until she finds it. We are required to be like that woman:

required to be the church that does not give up, sweeping away religiosity and seeking to reconnect with those who have lost their beliefs.

We will not need a lamp – instead we ask the Holy Spirit to guide and lead us in our prayers and conversations. It may be a Holy Spirit revelation to be shared in a greasy café. It may be the Holy Spirit equips us to understand the root of an issue needing resolution. It may be a Holy Spirit conviction to begin with an apology. It may simply be the Holy Spirit leading us to invite someone back into our community. The Holy Spirit is at work because God is committed.

And when people come back to Jesus, we celebrate!

153 fish and a recommitment

I cannot believe they do not recognize Jesus on the beach.

Out on the Sea of Galilee maybe they are busy, focused upon their fishing. It isn't until the mysterious figure tells them to cast their nets on the other side of the boat and they have caught a humungous catch, that they realize it is Jesus. It was some catch: 153 fish.

Peter knows the man on the beach is Jesus. At that moment of comprehension Peter cannot wait for the boat to get to shore. He dives into the water to swim to be with Jesus as quickly as he can.

The setting is beautiful: Jesus is cooking fish on the beach as the sun begins to rise and, then, as the other disciples join them, Jesus turns to Peter.

Three times Peter had denied Jesus. He had lost faith.

But then, on a beach in Galilee, he is asked:

'Do you love me?'

'Do you love me?'

'Do you love me?'

Three times. And three times Peter publicly commits to Jesus. A picture of forgiveness, of redemption and of hope for us all. Jesus had not given up on Peter. He, in fact, re-commissions him: 'Feed my lambs'; 'Take care of my sheep'; 'Feed my sheep.'

God is more committed to each of us than we ever can be to him.

Let's keep finding faith.

Bibliography

Adams, D., *The Salmon of Doubt* (London: Macmillan, 2002).

Barna, G., *Revolution* (Carol Stream, Illinois: Tyndale House Publishers, 2005).

Boyd, G.A., & Boyd, E.K., *Letters from a Skeptic: A Son Wrestles with His Father's Questions about Christianity* (Colorado Springs: David C. Cook, 2008).

Cameron, K.S., & Quinn, R.E., *Diagnosing and Changing Organizational Culture: Based on the Competing Values Framework* (San Francisco: Jossey-Bass, 2006).

Capon, R.F., *The Astonished Heart* (Grand Rapids, Michigan: Eerdmans Publishing, 1996).

Chalke, S., & Mann, A., *The Lost Message of Jesus* (Grand Rapids, Michigan: Zondervan, 2003).

Claiborne, S., *The Irresistible Revolution* (Grand Rapids: Zondervan, 2006).

Collins, J., *Good to Great* (London: Random House, 2001).

Drane, J., *The McDonaldization of the Church* (London: Darton, Longman & Todd, 2000).

Ekblad, B., *Reading the Bible with the Damned* (Louisville: Westminster John Knox Press, 2005).

Francis, L.J., & Richter, P., *Gone for Good? Church-Leaving and Returning in the Twenty-First Century* (Peterborough: Epworth, 2007).

Fowler, J., *Stages of Faith: The Psychology of Human Development and Quest for Meaning* (San Francisco: Harper, 1995).

Greig, P., *God on Mute: Engaging the Silence of Unanswered Prayer* (Eastbourne: Kingsway, 2007).

Hardy, C., *Understanding Organizations* (London: Penguin Books, 1999).

Holway, J.D., *Sermons on Several Occasions by the Reverend John Wesley* (Ilkeston: Moorleys, 1987).

Jamieson, A., *A Churchless Faith: Faith Journeys Beyond the Churches* (London: SPCK, 2002).

Kinnaman, D. & Lyons, G., *UnChristian: What a new generation really thinks about Christianity . . . and why it matters* (Grand Rapids, Michigan: Baker Books, 2007).

Lavan, G., ed., *Che Guevara Speaks: Selected Speeches and Writings* (New York: Pathfinder Press, 1967).

Lewis, C.S., *Mere Christianity* (London: Fount, 1997).

Marin, A., *Love is an Orientation: Elevating the Conversation with the Gay Community* (Downers Grove, Illinois: IVP, 2009).

McLaren, B.D., *Finding Faith: A Self-Discovery Guide for Your Spiritual Quest* (Grand Rapids, Michigan: Zondervan, 1999).

McLaren, B.D., *The Secret Message of Jesus: Uncovering the Truth That Could Change Everything* (Nashville: Thomas Nelson, 2006).

Miller, D., & MacMurray, J., *To Own a Dragon: Reflections on Growing Up Without a Father* (Colorado Springs: NavPress, 2006).

Newbigin, L., *The Gospel in a Pluralist Society* (Grand Rapids, Michigan: WCC Publications, 1989).

Nouwen, H.J.M., *Life of the Beloved* (New York: The Crossroad Publishing, 1992).

Tickle, P., *The Great Emergence: How Christianity Is Changing and Why* (Grand Rapids, Michigan: Baker Books, 2008).

Watters, E., *Urban Tribes: A Generation Redefines Friendship, Family, and Commitment* (New York: Bloomsbury, 2003).

Webber, R.E., *Ancient-Future Evangelism* (Grand Rapids, Michigan: Baker Books, 2003).

Willard, D., *Renovation of the Heart* (Colorado Springs: NavPress, 2002).

Endnotes

1   Luke 22:57.
2   Matthew 26:72. Though it may not be obvious from the NIV the term Peter used was a Judaic oath.
3   Matthew 26:74.
4   Adams, *The Salmon of Doubt*.
5   Nouwen, *Life of the Beloved*, pp. 22–23.
6   Webber, *Ancient-Future Evangelism*, p. 41.
7   Lewis, *Mere Christianity*, p. 153.
8   Drane, *McDonaldization*, p. 33.
9   Willard, *Renovation of the Heart*, p. 94.
10 Greig, *God on Mute*, p. 19.
11 Malcolm Gladwell, 'The Coolhunt'. http://www.gladwell.com/1997
12 Hardy, *Understanding Organizations*, p. 180.
13 Cameron & Quinn, *Diagnosing and Changing*, pp. 53–57.
14 http://www.charlesmore.com/cms/files/Starbucks_chairman_warns_of_the_commoditization_of_the_Starbucks_ID2218.pdf.
15 Capon, *The Astonished Heart*.
16 Tickle, *The Great Emergence*, p. 101.
17 Marin, *Love is an Orientation*, p. 38.
18 Jennifer Ashley, 'So you say your friend is gay', *Relevant Magazine* (July 2009).

[19] Marin, *Love is an Orientation*, p. 107.

[20] Three out of the fifty-member church have since died; two of cancer.

[21] Fowler, *Stages of Faith*.

[22] Jamieson, *A Churchless Faith*, p. 110.

[23] McLaren, *Finding Faith*, pp. 63–81.

[24] Ekblad, *Reading the Bible*, p. 4.

[25] Watters, *Urban Tribes*, p. 37.

[26] Claiborne, *The Irresistible Revolution*, p. 117.

[27] www.urbandictionary.com.

[28] Carl Beech (Christian Vision for Men), 'Men and the Church', Influence Conference, 13 March 2009.

[29] www.critical-mass.info.

[30] Watters, *Urban Tribes*, p. 109.

[31] Lavan, *Che Guevara*, p. 159.

[32] McLaren, *The Secret Message*, p. 29.

[33] http://www.guardian.co.uk/commentisfree/belief/2009/jun/25/environmentalism-religion

[34] Ruth Gledhill, 'Churchgoing on its knees as Christianity falls out of favour', *The Times* (9 May 2008).

[35] Collins, *Good to Great*, p. 86.